SPIRAL

SPIRAL

A MEMOIR OF HEALING AND
UNEARTHING THE GIFTS
WITHIN COMPLEX TRAUMA

SAMALA BYGRAVES

NEW DEGREE PRESS
COPYRIGHT © 2023 SAMALA BYGRAVES
All rights reserved.

SPIRAL
A Memoir of Healing and Unearthing the Gifts within Complex Trauma

ISBN	979-8-88926-638-9	*Paperback*
	979-8-88926-640-2	*Hardcover*
	979-8-88926-639-6	*Ebook*

For my children—the parts of my heart that live outside of me.

Table of Contents

AUTHOR'S NOTE		9
CHAPTER 1.	GATHERING ME	13
CHAPTER 2.	ROOTS	23
CHAPTER 3.	HUNGER	33
CHAPTER 4.	THE SPLIT	45
CHAPTER 5.	MAIDENHOOD	61
CHAPTER 6.	SOUL SKIN	81
CHAPTER 7.	RUNNING	89
CHAPTER 8.	THE CHOICE	103
CHAPTER 9.	BLOOD	119
CHAPTER 10.	DEAD HEADING	133
CHAPTER 11.	PERMISSION TO FEAST	145
CHAPTER 12.	RIGHTEOUS RAGE	157
CHAPTER 13.	THE CRACKED VESSEL	169
CHAPTER 14.	UNTETHERING	181
CHAPTER 15.	SIFTING THROUGH DEAD BODIES	193
EPILOGUE: UNFURLING		201
ACKNOWLEDGMENTS		205

Author's Note

present tense, and my reflection, I've included time stamps, so you my story. All names have been c who wanted theirs to stay the sam

This is a memoir of my spiritual, p formation. I share my story becau: our own stories, we open space fo and share theirs. And like Kali, have the daggers to the cut the tie to speak our individual truths.

Samala x

Spiraling,
Turning inward
Moving outward
Uncovering the gifts
Alchemizing fear
Into radiance
Returning home
Where it all began
Spiraling inward
Spiraling outward

A little over two years ago, I spiraled to the very bottom of a ravine. There, the crushing weight of an ocean of pain pushed me, not into physical death but into a rebirth. Choosing to live meant facing the darkness, the shadow, and the unseen parts of myself. And the hungry ghosts that had been traversing the depths of my being were waiting to be fed and welcomed into the light.

This story is as much a beginni
share my experience of discove
anxiety, eating disorder, and otl
offer my healing journey and dis
the narrative that currently exist:
over the coming pages is a story (
awakening to the wisdom that li
challenging and sometimes pain
I know it may be hard to read at
the end of this story.

When I began writing *Spiral*, the
my dreams often. She appeared
gers so I could cut the heavy ties
She showed me liberation and
side if I was willing to take the j
be forgiven, to dissolve the emc
and to see the gifts nestled with

Every experience we have is sto
we can later access the pearl of
then release the grains of sand tl
is not a linear process but rather
back to and unlocking the isola
sacred journey is to remember th
healed, and we are already who
unraveling, we come to know th
home is a gift, a sacred journey

I have chosen to write *Spiral* in
three timelines: the timeline o
past tense, the timeline before

CHAPTER 1

Gathering Me

―――

In order to remember
You had to first forget

A three-year-old girl cries out with all her might, "Mummy, please. Mummy, please come back. Mummy, please. Please. Please." Until she falls silent. Fists held tightly by her sides. Her heart pounding. She cannot move. She is all alone as she looks around at the trees, the dirt, and the sky.

WALES, NOVEMBER 2021—AGE THIRTY-THREE

I sank down, deeper and deeper into a state of calm and peace. As I did, my body began to shake and a hidden anguish bubbled to the surface, as did the intense discomfort of lying still. I noticed how afraid my body still was. Fearful thoughts intruded in on this quiet space. *Don't just lie here. This is unsafe. You have so much to do. Move, move, move.* But I didn't. I stayed as still as possible on the bed and continued with the subconscious reprogramming meditation.

Lana's voice came through the headphones. "Follow your breath down: five, four, three, two, one."

Slowly inhaling and exhaling, I followed my breath, like a weaving snake, down into the basement of my mind and breathed deeply into the darkness.

"There is nothing to fear," Lana said softly. "Call on your higher self to be your guide in whatever form they may take."

A little girl was walking next to me. I paused for a moment to look down at her. She was soft in the face and her big blue eyes looked up into mine. Her golden hair moved gently around her face in the soft breeze. She was wearing a lace rose-pink dress with frills for sleeves and ivory white fairy wings with a gold trim on her back. I knew her but didn't at the same time.

"What does your subconscious want to show you?" Lana's voice prompted.

The little girl intertwined her hand in mine and led me to a large arched metal door. Light shined through the sliver of space around it.

My heart beat rapidly, and somewhere I sensed tears running down my face. I stood for a few moments and then pressed my hand against the door. As my hand made contact, a blinding light engulfed me.

"What memory needs to be felt completely and reprocessed?" Lana prompted.

As the light faded, I looked around and saw something, or someone, in the distance. I was pulled toward that direction, so I began to walk.

As I got closer, I saw a little girl. A part of me recoiled, and a voice said, "No, don't go there," but I kept walking and arrived just behind her. She was still, as if a statue. She wasn't wearing any shoes; her feet were dirty, and her dress was in tatters. Her hands were clenched by her sides, and I noticed bits of dirt, snot, and tears dried on them. I recognized her as myself.

Gently I said, "Samala?" as I moved around to her side slowly and knelt.

She didn't reply and breathed quietly. Every so often, a sob caught in her throat. Her eyes were fixed ahead, and I softly placed my hand on her shoulder. She felt so cold to touch.

"Samala, what are you doing?" I asked.

She didn't move her gaze.

"I'm waiting for Mummy," she whispered.

"What do you need now to heal and reprocess this memory?" Lana asked.

I moved around to face her on my knees in the dirt, and I softened my body toward hers.

"What do you need?" I asked.

She was quiet for some time, and then she peeked a look at me. In that moment, our eyes met. Her pain, her fear, her confusion, her sadness, and her deep rejection moved like waves through my entire body.

"I want my mummy. I want her to come back. I want her to love me," she cried.

I opened my arms to her, and she moved forward into my lap.

"It's okay," I said as I gently smoothed her hair with my hand. She rested her body against mine, her exhaustion leaking away as she softened.

"Samala, it's time to come away from here now. I'm so sorry I didn't come sooner," I whispered on the top of her head.

She looked up at me with trepidation.

"But what if she comes back for me. What if she comes back to get me, and I'm not here?"

"She's not coming," I said. "But I am here. I love you, and we are more than enough."

A little sob left her, but she got up off my lap and put her hand out to take mine. I saw the metal door shimmering up ahead. As we walked toward our exit, I looked down to see her smiling. As we walked through the door, she slowly dissolved into me.

"Take all the time you need to fully feel what you witnessed, and come back up when you are ready," Lana said.

The binaural beats faded, and after some time I was back in the present moment, back in the room. I wiggled my toes and fingers. I knew my face, neck, and chest were wet. My body was heavy with exhaustion as I sat up on the bed. I took my headphones off, wrapped my arms around my body, and cried.

The tears were cleansing, especially after nearly three years of not being able to cry. These deep meditative sessions have enabled me to travel down into the depths of my subconscious. Sometimes I can't access anything, but slowly all the memories have been coming back.

For as long as I could remember, I believed something was inherently wrong with me. I was an overly anxious and highly stressed person. I did not think I had experienced trauma. Trauma was for people who experienced extreme disastrous circumstances like war and earthquakes. I somehow forgot about all the other traumas, such as physical, sexual, and emotional. And all those traumas happened to me.

My mind had been so clever at hiding the truth, but eventually, my mind and body reached their breaking point when I woke in the middle of the night having made the decision that I was going to end my life. I had gone on as long as I could, existing in a state of toxic chronic stress. I was always "on edge," despite my outward positive disposition, and inside I was readying myself for disaster. My therapist had likened my mind to a submarine, and my periscope was permanently above water looking out for danger. My baseline was either fight, flight, or freeze when things really got on top of me. By 2020, it seemed that everything was collapsing around me, no matter how hard I attempted to control my life.

The suicidal ideation was a catalyst, and it catapulted me into what would become my time to heal and be reborn. On that dark night, in the depths of my despair, a doorway opened for me. This doorway had always been open, since I was a small child, and I always felt an undercurrent of protection, despite the circumstances. I was looked after; I was guided. My inner voice, my light, always shining, even in the darkest of moments. When I think of how my life could have gone, I always found a way back to myself. I always found a way back home. And this time, I was staying.

Recalling memories from traumatic experiences can be slippery. Like sand slipping through the cracks of your fingers, despite how tightly you hold them together. When a traumatic experience or perceived threat occurs, the brain can't always file that memory away in chronological order. Sometimes it is deeply buried within the subconscious or broken up into fragments. There can be large gaps in memories or periods of "blankness."

The release of cortisol and adrenaline can affect the way we feel the pain of the experience in real time, which is useful in life-or-death situations. However, when the perceived threat or real threat is occurring daily, the mind and body may have no choice but to move into survival mode, suppressing emotional trauma deep in the body. As I spent more time relaxing my body and began to feel safe in it, the memories and my perception of those past experiences began to surface along with the physical pain. My body and mind slowly revealed the truth to me.

It took me some months to be able to relive the most poignant traumatic memories and process them. The first step was facing the truth. I had to take ownership of myself and my part to play in it. I was no longer interested in being a victim. I had to be responsible for my healing. For most of my life, I had been waiting for someone to show up and "save me," but the truth—and the lesson I have repeatedly learned—is that it always had to be me. I had to give myself the love and safety I had never received. I had to gather myself, hold myself, and reparent myself. I had to journey into the darkest of places and shine my love there. If not for me, for my children.

WESTERN AUSTRALIA, 1990—AGE THREE

Something dark in my dreams. A nightmare, a dream gone wrong. Am I all alone? Is anyone in the house? My eyes open to black velvet; shadows move across the wall with sharp teeth and hollow eyes. I cry loudly. Then footsteps sound along the hall and come into the room. Someone is there, and then, arms are around me. I reach out hesitantly to place a hand on either side of the face I find; it's bearded and as I pat up and down, I know it's my dad. "Daddy," I say and wrap my arms around his neck. My small body is safe in his embrace as he rocks me back to sleep.

Later that day, I stand behind my dad and circle my arms around his grounded legs as glass shatters all around me. I take a quick look through and see her launch another attack.

"She's *evil*," my mum screams. She is twisted and rageful, but even though she scares me, I still want her.

"She's a three-year-old, Deb. She's not evil. She just a three-year-old," my dad says in a low voice.

My eyes widen as she hurls words I don't understand, but I know they mean something. She puts her ammo down, but she's not ready to give up yet. I move closer to my shield. My hands grasp the fabric of his jeans, and he becomes the wall between us—my mum and me.

He turns around and scoops me up, carrying me out of the war zone and into the quiet openness. The sun beats down as I squint my eyes. I hear the echoes of my mother's incomprehensible anger coming from the house.

I get down from his arms and run to play underneath the trees. Jasmine scents the wind, and my bare feet soon turn red from the earth.

I take a stick and start jabbing it into the dirt, making a hole, bigger and bigger. *I'm going to dig to the center.* Tiny ants crawl toward my cave, and I push the jagged end of the stick into one. It's strangely satisfying, so I squash another and another. Soon, the cave becomes a mass grave for dead ants. I look up to see my dad watching me. His face looks strange, crumpled almost, and something inside me turns over. I run to him, and I place my hands on either side of his face.

"Don't be sad, Daddy." I wrap my arms around his neck.

WALES, FEBRUARY 2020—AGE THIRTY-TWO

I looked at the tomato sauce splattered across the kitchen floor. *Did I do that?* The sound of crying caught my awareness, and I looked over to see that it's my two-year-old daughter Isla. I looked down to see four-month-old Meredith looking up at me, wide-eyed in my arms.

What is happening? Where did I go? I felt as though I was hovering over myself, and if you were to look at me, I would have been flickering. As drew Isla to me, I picked up on her slight hesitancy, and my heart broke at this. I started to cry, and she wrapped her arms around my neck.

"Don't cry, Mummy. It's okay."

I wrapped my arms around Isla, gathering my girls closer to me as a voice deep inside spread its cold fingers around my heart and whispered, *Evil.*

CHAPTER 2

Roots

As a child,
I would look up to the sun
Soaking up the warmth
As it spread across my face
Feeling held, warm and safe

Tall blue gums stretch far above me as I run as fast as I can, darting in between them. The spinifex bushes threaten to catch my skin, but I dodge their itchy sting.

WESTERN AUSTRALIA, 1990—AGE THREE
I look at the gumtrees through the window of my parents' Toyota Ute as we rush past them. They stand tall, like giant stick men, with their shaggy hair drooping down toward the red earth. I watch nervously as the road transforms from tarmac to gray gravel. I hear the tires crunch over the dirt road and look out at the dust cloud surrounding the Ute. Rubbing fresh tears from my face, I ask, "Where are we going, Mummy," but I get no answer.

Panic swells like a tide in my chest as it moves up toward my throat. I make myself small and sink deeper into the seat. I glance between her seat and the side of the car. I see her white knuckled hands grip the steering wheel. She says nothing, but I can sense her anger seeping from the front of the car back to me like invisible tendrils wrapping themselves around my body. My stomach spins as I look out the window at the arid bushland that could belong to no other place but Australia.

I know we are very far from my house, and I start crying. I reach down with my fingers and nervously pick my belly button.

The Ute comes to a stop. If it wasn't for the sound of my crying, it would be peaceful. I watch her take the keys out of the ignition, open her door, and get out. I wail even louder as she walks around to my door. As she opens it, I look up at her. I search her face, but she's not there. Her eyes are dark, and her face is red.

"Get out," she says.

"No," I say. "No, no, no, Mummy, no." I tightly hold onto the seat belt, but she pulls my hands off the slippery material.

I know now for certain that I am in *big* trouble. She leans over and unbuckles the clip. Frantically, I grab anything I can as she yanks me out of the Ute and into the wide open. Wordless screams and cries begin to pour from my mouth.

Dizziness hits me as she puts me down on the ground. I stand still for a moment but then follow her as she walks quickly back to the driver side door.

"Mummy, please. Mummy, please. I'll be good, Mummy, please," I sob, as I pull at her clothes.

But she pushes me back, opens her door, and gets into the driver seat. She closes the door, and I cry even harder. *She's leaving me.* I claw at the door, and then place my hands flat as they slide down the body of the Ute as she slowly drives away. I begin to run behind but stop as gravel and dust fly back into my eyes.

I stop crying and become still. My eyes widen and my hands turn to little fists by my sides as I watch the Ute and my mum vanish around the corner.

WALES, FEBRUARY 2020—AGE THIRTY-TWO
I woke up in the dead of the night. My four-month-old baby Meredith lay tucked against my breast, feeding gently. I leaned down to smell her sweet smell. Tears slid down my cheeks as I breathed her in.

Jumbled thoughts bounced around my head. *I must be better, for Isla, for Luke, for Meredith. I must be better.*

But I can't. I did it again. I got angry. Isla was having a tantrum, Meredith was screaming in my arms, and I couldn't take it. In the pressure of it all, I yelled so loudly, and when I looked at their little faces, they were scared. I can't do it anymore.

I don't want to be like her. They will be better without me. They'll be safer and happier without me because I am broken, I'm evil, I'm a monster.

In the darkness, the thoughts, like electric shocks, ricocheted throughout my body. I couldn't take it anymore. I sat up slightly on my elbow, my heart pounding as I heard the familiar sound of the train on the tracks behind my house. My mind began to form a plan. *The train track is just there. It would be over in a moment. I can't hurt them anymore if I am dead.* I slid Meredith away from me and moved to sit on the side of the bed. I placed my feet flat on the floor and inhaled deeply.

I thought, *I'll miss them so much, but I'll be dead, so I won't feel it. I won't feel anything. It will be okay. This is the right thing; this is the brave thing. People don't kill themselves for themselves. They do it for those they love.*

I didn't want to be a burden anymore, and I didn't want my children to grow up with a broken mother. I wanted them to remember a mother who loved them. Meredith whimpered and tears started rolling down my face. My body responded to her cry, as milk trickled down my stomach.

She won't take a bottle, I thought.

But she'll have to, said another voice.

I stood up. Should I get changed? Did it matter?

I was going to kill myself, and with that recognition, I spiraled. I dropped to my knees and cried. I did my best to contain the howl that was desperate to leave my body. I didn't want to wake up the soundly sleeping baby.

I am going to do this. I have to.

I felt such conviction in that thought, but then, a moment later, a warm glow began moving within. A resounding *no* echoed through me, a voice that was not so different from my own. *You are not going to kill yourself because this isn't you.*

Calm washed over me, and I thought, *If this isn't me, who am I?*

Something deep within me told me to get back into bed and deal with that tomorrow. As I lay back down, I drew Meredith into me. Her tiny hands curled around my fingers, and I knew it was time to feed her again. As my baby suckled softly into the night, I whispered, "Thank you."

The Australian outback was my backyard. I belonged to the bush, the burnt reds, oranges, and silvery greens of the desert. To the rusty smell of the dirt. To the fat tadpoles begging to be caught when the rain came. To the snakes that needed to be outrun. I belonged to the earth, and it belonged to me.

As a child, I never feared the outback but the inside of my own home—the nightmares that would come in the middle of the night. The cold looks, the back of a hand, and the weight of a body. The gaping wound that was continually opened and poked, blistered. I learned how to cover it well. I morphed and shifted, shape changing to suit those I needed for survival.

The experience by the roadside is the first memory I hold of my mother. That moment and so many others were seared into my mind and my body. They rippled and spread like black ink throughout the entire fabric of my being. From those moments, perceptions formed. And then followed the beliefs. *You are not safe* and *You are not wanted* echoed through every cell in my body. The thick wall of protection went up around me, only to be fortified as time went on and experiences overlaid each other like a mottled scar.

The day after I hit what I can only describe as a point of no return in February 2020, I called a therapist who had been recommended to me by a friend. I had known that something was not right, but I waited, as sometimes people do, for things to get bad before I did something. I did not know what I needed nor did I understand what was happening to me, but I felt an awareness that something had shifted within me. I was unraveling, and there was a level of inertia to it. I was being pulled inward and felt a burning desire to remember something.

WALES, MARCH 16, 2020—AGE THIRTY-TWO

I sat down in an armchair as Liz followed me into the room and closed the door. I looked around the room and thought, *This is nice. It's light and open.* I could see the blue sky through the window, and I gazed at the birds that flew by. My attention was brought back to the moment by Liz, who handed me a plastic cup of water. She sat down across from me.

"Okay, Samala, I know we spoke on the phone, and you mentioned some of the things that you were experiencing. Would you like to talk more about how you are feeling?" she said and took a notepad and pen from the side table

"Well, I don't want to feel anxious anymore. That night, the night before I called you, I wanted to kill myself. I don't want to, not really. I mean sometimes I think my children would be better off without me, but I also don't want to do that to them either." I looked down as I said this.

I didn't really know what else to say, but I went on. "I guess I just want to feel normal. I want to be a good mum. I don't want to get angry. Sometimes, sometimes I do things like eat a lot and then make myself sick. Like not all the time but sometimes."

"Okay, I understand. I'm going to ask you a few more questions regarding how you are feeling and behaviors. And then we'll go from there. Okay?"

I nodded.

At the end of the session, I left with a "diagnosis." But over time that diagnosis would change because in that first session I only spoke about the present—the anxiety, my eating habits, suicidal thoughts. I said nothing of my childhood or even my life before this point. I left with a diagnosis for an eating disorder and chronic anxiety. That was going to be the point of where I began my recovery. At the time, I still believed I needed to be "fixed." However, all those things were symptoms of a deeper underlying root cause. Bringing what was living in my unconscious out into my conscious self was an integral part of my transformation.

Before 2020, I knew I'd experienced things that weren't "nice," but the memories were jumbled. A snapshot here, a feeling there, but I had blocked out the majority of what had happened to me. Of what I did remember, I made excuses. I pushed it away and down into my body. I couldn't verbalize everything that had happened, but when I began talking about my childhood, my entire body would shake and the back of my head would pound. Slowly over 2020, and in the years to follow, I was able to pull apart the cobwebs. To *see* with open eyes that what had happened to me was traumatic and was also complex.

It wasn't just about my relationship with my mother, as there were many strands to pull, and I began to unravel the root cause as to why I was triggered into stress, anxiety, and fear at almost every turn. A smell, a loud noise, a look from someone, even a song could send me into an anxiety attack within moments. The multiple traumas, and not just in the home, contributed to my brain associating multiple everyday things as dangerous. By the time I ended up meeting with my therapist, it was like opening mountains of mystery boxes. I had no idea what was going to be inside.

SAMALA'S JOURNAL—APRIL 2020
"Facing up to this is hard. I'm scratching at the surface, and I'm very scared of what I'm going to find."

AUSTRALIA, MID-TO-EARLY 1990S—AGE FOUR OR FIVE

Muffled screams escape as I gasp for air. Her body presses mine down into the floor. My head is underneath her chest. My eyes are forced shut and everything is black and stars. She screams wordless fury at me as I resist her. Frantically, I make weak fists with my hands and pound at her sides. I try to wriggle my body out from underneath her. She won't move.

"Mummy, I can't breathe," I cry out from underneath her. "Mummy. I can't breathe."

Underneath the diagnosis was an adult who had experienced multiple forms of trauma. And like scar tissue, it wasn't solely about what had happened to me but what was happening within that was continuing to grow thick and knotted, embedded in everything by the time I had reached that moment in 2020.

The dynamic between my mother and me was a dark secret that I had skirted around. Not only that, but I found it difficult to maintain friendships and relationships and had found myself in relationships mirroring similar dynamics to that of my childhood. I struggled with intimate relationships and friendships, and I people pleased and subordinated to other people's needs as a way of survival.

All the while, a rage and anger grew within, and I lived with a constant knot in my stomach. I was filled with self-loathing and a belief that I was a burden to everyone who loved me. Even then, I did not believe people really loved or even liked me. So many of my beliefs about myself and other people were intertwined with a lopsided perception born out of my past experiences.

SAMALA'S JOURNAL—APRIL 2020
"There's a feeling of… standing on the edge of something. I want to connect with the wider fabric of my being."

A realization began to unfold along with a conviction that I had to change the way I perceived myself and my experiences. I was slowly awakening to myself and my truth. I wanted to see all the shadows and darkness that existed within me. As I sifted through the experiences with Liz, and those who followed and supported my healing and transformation, it was as though I was turning back in time.

A burning desire to travel to the root of my being and touch the heart of the pain ignited. To release the ghosts of my younger selves that were still roaming the basement of my mind. To slowly peel away the layers of misperception that obscured the truth and wisdom my most painful experiences had to offer. I was finally ready to embark on my own heroine's journey.

I was finally ready to begin the journey back to myself.

CHAPTER 3

Hunger

―

I emerged from the womb
Hungry
Born desiring
A child dreaming
Gathering to me
Treasures, and Magic
Always searching
For the fairy ring
Take me away
As a ravenous hunger ripped through me

SAMALA'S JOURNAL—MARCH 2020
"A lethargy comes over me and thoughts form such as, What's the point? And then the hunger comes. The ravenous hunger, and I am so empty. I will consume everything. But it's too late. It's too late for me. That's what the thoughts say."

WALES, MARCH 16, 2020—AGE THIRTY-TWO

I parked my car on Adelaide Street. I had arrived fifteen minutes early. But that was me. I could never be late. I also never understood how people managed to be "on time." My stomach gurgled wildly. I tried to work out what I would say to Liz. I knew I needed to talk about the suicidal thoughts, and I supposed, the eating issues. But beyond that, my mind went blank.

When I had called her weeks before, I had said, "Something is wrong. My anxiety is out of control. I'm feeling suicidal, and I just want to be a good mum to my kids." But then, moments before I was going to meet with her, I couldn't verbalize the feelings of dread and darkness that were rising like a tidal wave. The darkness took me over and turned me into my worst nightmare. Despite feeling a moment of calm after deciding not to end my life, it didn't take long for the daily pain and suffering to return. Something was different, yes, as though I possessed an awareness that wasn't there before, but it was drowned out by the war going on inside of me.

My attention was brought back to the to the BBC news playing on the car radio. Prime Minister Boris Johnson was expected to make an announcement that evening as to whether the UK was going to go into a nationwide lockdown to flatten the "curve" of the fast-approaching pandemic. I secretly hoped he would. I wanted life to pause.

I got out of the car and walked down the street. It was warm for the time of year in the UK, and I was pleased to be greeted by a late afternoon blue sky. As I walked down the road, a corner shop caught my eye. I felt a surge of adrenaline and wondered if I had time to buy chocolate. But I resisted and instead walked into a charity shop. I flicked through dresses, feeling the quality of the material with my fingers. I found an ivy green cotton dress and bought it. I didn't like it much, but I needed to do something to distract myself from the storm raging in my mind.

I crossed the street and wondered how many other people were feeling how I did. I was in a bubble, and no one else could get in. It was just me in my bubble of pain. I located her door and rang the buzzer. Moments later, I was greeted by a tall, blonde, and warm-looking woman. She welcomed me into her room and gestured me toward the empty chair. I sat down, as my throat and courage coiled tighter and smaller within me.

AUSTRALIA, 1994—AGE SEVEN
"Samala, get back here *right now*!" Mum yells.

I run into my bedroom, shut the door, and climb into the wardrobe. I reach into a bottom drawer and pull out stale white bread and shove it into my mouth. I close my eyes. The bread feels sticky in my mouth, but I keep eating. I keep eating and eating and eating until she finds me, but by then I am full and numb.

When I was around seven, I started hiding slices of white bread in my bottom drawer. I'd return to them at times of distress, such as shouting, arguments, or after being hit. I would curl up in my wardrobe, close my eyes, and focus on eating. My breath ragged and heavy, slowly my heart rate would come down and I could breathe again. Food became a source comfort but also a source of focus as it became something I never seemed to have enough of. I always wanted more.

When my parents threw dinner parts, I would stand in the kitchen, knowing I would be sent to bed. My mother made the most delicious chocolate mousse and served it in beautiful, wide champagne glasses. In the morning, after the parties, I would sneak into the kitchen and run my finger around the rims of the glasses just to get a taste before they were washed clean. Food, like her, was unpredictable. Sometimes, I would come home and she would have made apple and cinnamon muffins, and other times, I would open my lunch box to find a single tomato. Food became black and white to me. If I was good, I got to eat. If I was bad, I didn't. If I was good, she loved me. If I was bad, she didn't.

I became curious of what other people ate and how much. What kind of treats did they get to have? As I grew up, all my emotions became tied up in food. It became a way to numb and escape what I was feeling, experiencing, and witnessing. I would also eat if I was excited or overstimulated. I became disconnected from my own body and its nourishment needs. As I entered teenagerhood, food and my body became a source of concern and control. I internalized the messages I saw modeled by the women and media around me. I was thirteen when I went on my first diet and became obsessed with eating perfectly and healthily. I would frequently ask my boyfriend, "Does my stomach look flat enough?"

If I ate something I perceived as "bad," a spiral of hateful thoughts would follow, and I would do something to compensate such as restricting or exercising. But over time, it escalated, going from bingeing to purging. Yes, it was to soothe and numb emotions, but it was more complex than a single reason. It was also a way to stay small. When my therapist asked why I wanted to be small, I said deep down I wanted to be small like a child, I didn't really want to be an adult, and I wanted to be small enough to be picked up and held.

The purge became a coping mechanism. For in the aftermath of the act, I would find myself back in my body, feeling something again. The numbing action of eating followed by the sharp awakening of self-harm was a viscous and addictive cycle. Not to mention the guilt and loathing that distracted me from the actual pain I was running from. Of course, it took a couple of decades before this would play out. As a child, I had no awareness of the ways I was choosing to self-soothe. It was completely impulsive.

Not long before my fourth birthday, my sister Una was born. My mother had to stay in the hospital for a little while, maybe a week, after her birth. While she was away, I pined for her; being away from her was far worse than anything that could happen when she was with me. My father and I put banners up. I wanted her to see what I had done. When she returned, she had a baby in her arms that she carried around and told me not to wake up, not to disturb, and not to touch. She cooed and coddled this baby while I would stare and experience waves of feelings I could not comprehend.

I observed my mother as if she were something to study. I watched how she was with other women and men. She'd say one thing to a friend's face but would say things about how they looked, their weight, or their position in life when they weren't around. I saw how she pinched at her body and the freezer full of Jenny Craig meals. I witnessed her frustration with me; I just took it to be the way things were. As I grew up, my experiences only compounded my perception that something was wrong with me, and my worth and importance came from outside sources.

Early on, I internalized the message that I was not enough. I began to seek validation through praise for being good and helpful, and then eventually with relationships, whether they were intimate or not. I rarely chose anyone or allowed myself to truly decide if something was what I wanted. I said yes to every invitation out of fear that I would not be accepted anywhere else or by anyone else. "You are not really wanted here" was a message that lived deep in my mind and heart.

After the first session with Liz, the UK was placed under a nationwide lockdown. I was concerned about how we would continue our work together, but we came up with the solution, which was our sessions would take place over the telephone. Most of our calls took place in my parked car just outside of my house because it was impossible to find any quiet moments with everyone "staying home." Paradoxically, really, I began the journey of my life in my parked car outside of my house, traveling nowhere and everywhere.

WALES, APRIL 26, 2020—AGE THIRTY-TWO

I accepted the call, and Liz's voice came through the speaker in my car.

"Hi, Samala, how are you?"

"I'm okay, thank you. How are you?"

"I'm really well. Okay, so I received your food diaries. Thank you for those. It looks like you had a difficult day on Sunday. Would you like to start the session there?"

"Um, okay. I guess there was a situation that upset me on Sunday." I paused. My throat stayed tight as I continued, "I was talking to my mum. She started recalling an Easter when I was three. She said she and Dad made a little Easter bunny box, and I was so excited about the box and the craft. She said I was so sweet, and I didn't even care about the chocolate. She just kept saying how lovely I was. How sweet I was. And it made me feel strange. Angry almost. Then something popped into my head. I thought, *Well why did you do all the awful things to me if you loved me so much?*" I stopped talking. *Dangerous territory,* a little voice in my head whispered.

"Okay, Samala, let's stop there for a moment. I have noticed over the last few sessions that you may want to talk about some things. Would you like to park the eating disorder work today and talk a little bit more about your mum?"

As time went on and we delved deeper into my past, I began to recognize that the eating disorder was a coping mechanism, which had done its best to protect me. In many ways, the anxiety had saved me. My anxiety had been ringing the alarm bell for nearly three decades. I was firefighting all the emotional pain with dysfunctional coping mechanisms, and the root cause was years and years of varied trauma even though I truly had no idea I was traumatized. While I knew my mother could be difficult, things hadn't been great, and stressful things had occurred in my life, a glass wall stood between me, the truth, and my feelings about those experiences.

When I read back through journals from when I was a teenager, I found entries where I had written "I don't want to be like her," but I couldn't *actually* put my finger on what "being like her" was. I began to see that my experience and perspective of her was different to other people's. And when it came to confronting the varied wounds, it was not easy telling people what had happened, especially those who were in my family unit. People have often asked, "Why didn't you say anything?" And my response has been, "I didn't feel safe."

WALES, APRIL 2020—AGE THIRTY-TWO
"Dad, the anxiety, the eating disorder, the suicidal thoughts are all symptoms of complex trauma," I said as I started picking at the side of my thumb, something I always did when I was nervous.

"But you look so healthy," my dad said over the phone. I could tell by his voice that he was shocked. I was sitting on the couch in the living room and leaned back into the pillow as I spoke.

"I'm very good at hiding things… and, Dad, that's not all. There's more," I said. I looked around as the shadows made patterns on the walls. It was early British summer time, and the sun shone brightly through the blinds on the window.

I had been dreading this conversation. I was comfortable with talking about my experience with anxiety. I was open about the fact that I took antidepressants, but the eating disorder and everything else that lay beneath was inconceivable. I knew was going to rock the very fabric of my family's disjointed foundation. I was speaking out about something we all knew, something we all skirted around, and something we all dealt with in our way. For years, I had even noticed how my dad receded into himself whenever my mother was around. I noticed how he tightened in her presence.

To everyone, including me, I pretended everything was normal—at family gatherings, birthdays, and events. I pretended everything was "fine." I made excuses for all the dysfunction, including my own, and ignored the gnawing "something is not right" sensation in the pit of my stomach.

In those early sessions with Liz, my eyes opened to the truth about the relationship between my mother and me. It was as though someone had switched a light on, and everything was there in an instant. What I had experienced was not normal nor was it okay. Most crucially, it was not my fault. That knowledge meant I couldn't continue as I was, and I had to finally, after all these years, use my voice and speak my truth.

But it wasn't easy. The "not my fault" not only needed to be recognized consciously but subconsciously. And that would take some time to really sink in and work through. I also had no idea how to be vulnerable. I had no idea who I was. I didn't have very many close friendships because I was terrified of rejection and abandonment.

While my mother had said she loved me, my perception of her actions said the opposite. I had believed my whole life that my mother's behavior was *my* fault. I spoke of it to no one because I believed if I told anyone what was happening, they would see the fault in me. They would think, *What is so broken in you that makes your mum treat you that way.*

I had known from a young age that my mother suffered with depression. I saw her go back and forth to a therapist. I had witnessed her asleep in bed for hours on end. I watched the anger and the tears, sensing the emptiness.

I had wondered why I was not a good enough motivation for her to change. I explained away her behavior and made it my fault, and eventually my responsibility. But when I did a 360 and looked at myself with my children, I knew I had a choice. I was going to heal and transform myself.

My father had always said to me, "You're okay. Aren't you, Samala? You're okay?" I believed I was being a good daughter and a good girl by not causing anyone any trouble or worry, so I would reply, "Yes, Dad, I'm fine." And the "I'm fine" became another mask.

When I told him about the suicidal thoughts, the eating disorder, and that I was essentially falling apart, the immense guilt that came at letting him down made me want to bottle it all up again. It was like a vulnerability hangover.

"Dad, the anxiety, the eating disorder, and the suicidal thoughts are all symptoms," I said.

"Of what?" he sounded confused.

"Of Mum, of how she was, what happened to me, and how she still is. I mean it's not all just Mum. It's everything, but I'm still living with unhealed trauma, Dad. My nervous system is in tatters." I struggled to bring the right words to name all the events and make it make sense.

"Dad, I've been abused; I was emotionally and physically abused by my own mother. I was sexually abused by a peer and then bullied by my peers. So many things, Dad. I have zero self-worth. Do you not see?" I was getting annoyed, surely, he *knew*. Did I have to explain it all to him? My defenses went up because I began to sense that people would rather believe these things didn't happen, or they weren't "that bad," especially when a parent was called into question. It was too hard to comprehend that a mother could be *unloving*.

"I'm going to continue working with a therapist to heal and work through all the trauma, Dad. It's not as simple as accepting what happened and moving on. It's all still in my body. It's all still playing out. I have never dealt with *any* of the awful things that happened to me. Do I have your support while I work through this?" I continued.

"Of course you do. I love you, and I just want you to be alright," he said, and I caught the sadness in his voice.

I could hear in his voice that guilt assailed him, and I knew he wished he could have done things differently. But I couldn't delay healing or continue silencing myself to preserve other people's feelings any longer.

A huge weight lifted as I began to speak my truth and put my own needs first. I had used the eating disorder as a way of suppressing my own needs and wants. It became a way of pushing all the uncomfortable emotions down and to dampen that desire to do and experience more.

But the more I used my voice, the more I listened to my body and metaphorically fed my intuition. I recognized a hunger was indeed within me—a lust for more and for creative expression. A hunger for life.

A hunger for *me*.

CHAPTER 4

The Split

―

Inside a childhood nightmare
Too exhausted to wake up
And see, that there is nothing here
Only a dream
That seems so real

When I was ten, my mother gave me a book called *Juniper* written by Monica Furlong. *Juniper* is the story of a Celtic princess, Ninnoc, who is sent to live with her godmother, Euny, a "wise woman" on the outskirts of the kingdom. She is to stay with her for a year and a day. Ninnoc learns the art of magic and healing among other things from Euny. Through this challenging initiation, she cultivates her own inner strength, magic, intuition, and connection to self in order to face and overcome the dark magic wielded by her aunt. Just like many other tales, such as *Vasilisa the Beautiful*, these young women are sent to meet the wild, normally in the form of the wise woman, and in the case of Vasilisa, Baba Yaga. In meeting the wild, they move through an initiation, connecting to their intuition and strength. Emerging as children no more but maidens on a journey to become women.

AUSTRALIA, NORTHERN TERRITORY, 1998—AGE TEN

I wonder what it would be like to be a part of a family who really loves each other.

I look over at a smiling family and ponder this. I turn my head back, and I am faced with the reality of my situation. I can see the anger and coldness forming like a dark cloud between my mum and dad. I want to be somewhere else.

AUSTRALIA, WESTERN AUSTRALIA, 1996—AGE EIGHT

Just after my eighth birthday, we moved from the goldfields in Western Australia to the lush, green farmland of a town two hours south of Perth. I was incredibly excited for this move. We would be closer to my nanna and grandad—my dad's parents—and my cousins who lived in Perth. Everything about this move filled me with anticipation, and we would also be closer to the beach.

The time spent there holds some of the happiest memories from my childhood. When I reflect, the memories are dreamlike. It was a period of respite. The soft bed rest I would sorely need. My parents appeared relatively happy—they fought less—and for the most part, my relationship with my mother was easier. I still saw signs of her absentness and the occasional bursts of anger or outrage, but I did my best to be good.

At times, I would still wake in the night in a cold sweat, having wet the bed or had a nightmare, but in the daytime, I forgot all about the night and dove into my newfound sense of freedom. I spent most of my time with the girl next door, who became my best friend. Meeting Amanda led me to begin horse riding on my horse, Carly-Beth.

AUSTRALIA, WESTERN AUSTRALIA 1996—AGE EIGHT

Opening the sliding doors, I skip out onto the veranda. Purply blue wisteria hangs down in huge drapes along the veranda roof, obscuring my vision to the back garden. As I walk under the wisteria, the garden expands around me. I stand under a large pine tree and look up. The branches are perfect for climbing. Just as I begin my ascent, I hear a girl's voice coming from the garden next to mine. Leaving the tree, I walk up to the edge of my garden.

As I near the fence, I notice a small hut made mostly of chicken wire. And soon after, I hear a chorus of squeaking. I see a girl sitting inside. She is talking to someone, or something, but I can't see what. A twig breaks underneath my foot, and she looks up. Our eyes meet, and she grins a wide-open smile. I smile back. She has big brown eyes, high cheek bones, and long straight brown hair. She stands up, and I notice she is cradling something in her arms. She holds a small, orange fluffy guinea pig out toward me. "This is Ginger," she says.

And from that moment on, we are inseparable.

AUSTRALIA, WESTERN AUSTRALIA, 1997—AGE NINE

Carly-Beth snorts as I pull on her reins and move her in a circle. Her hooves grind into the dirt and grass. Tears, dirt, and dust stick to my face as I speak relentlessly to her.

"I'll be happy to leave you. I'm glad I'm leaving you. I'll be better off with you. You're a bad horse. You never do what you're told. I can't wait to have to not ride you anymore," I say as tears flow.

I breathe jaggedly. My heart is breaking, and embarrassment, shame, and anger all merge into one. I trot her over to her trailer and jump off. I tie up her reins and begin to take off her tack. Then I stop and bury my face in her neck. I breathe in her earthy smell. I love her so much.

Tears sting my eyes as I think about what just happened and how panic had overtaken me the moment I entered the jump arena. I couldn't remember where the numbers were or the order of the jumps, and as soon as I panicked, so did Carly-Beth. Our combined panic sent her manic, and she bolted out of the arena.

I smooth her mane and lean against her. Anger and the unfairness of my life swells. The embarrassment of messing up a competition stings, but the realization that this is my last weekend away with her because we were leaving Western Australia and moving to the Northern Territory cuts deeply.

Thoughts tumble forward as I stand there. I am desperate not to leave, but how do I tell my parents? I know things aren't okay. I know my parents aren't okay, and I can't escape the feeling of impending doom. I don't want to start a new school; I don't want to make new friends, and I don't want to leave Carly-Beth. Eventually, I stand back and brush her down while I wait for Amanda and her mum to find me.

I would have done anything for Carly-Beth. I would get up early before school and head out to clear out her stable, feed, and water her. Even on the coldest of mornings, I would jump over the fence and run down to meet her, cracking the ice on her water bucket. There I would wrap my arms around her neck and feel her gentle heartbeat, my heart slowing to match hers. Being with her exposed an untapped part of me. When Carly-Beth and I were galloping over fields, I would spread my arms wide like wings, and in those moments, I was unstoppable.

But that all came crashing down when I found out we were moving. I didn't even go to say goodbye to her when we left. I didn't know what to do with the insurmountable grief boiling within, and instead I buried it deeply. In the months to come, I would wake up, having dreamt of her, desperate to feel her close and ride her one more time. I slept with the only photo I had of her under my pillow until it was crumpled and worn.

We moved to a remote island in the Gulf of Carpentaria, where you could only live if you worked there or were family of someone who worked there. We were there for less than a year, but it marked the beginning of a deeply challenging time of my life. It was where I would begin the lesson of self-sufficiency as the very bedrock of my foundation was split and separated into fractured pieces.

AUSTRALIA, NORTHERN TERRITORY, SEPTEMBER 1997—AGE TEN

I smile at the flight attendant as she says goodbye and guides me out of the plane. As I step out of the door and onto the metal ladder, a wall of heat slams into my body. I bring my hand to cover my eyes as they adjust to the glaring sunlight. As the haze of heat clears, I see two tin sheds with an awning connecting them. *Must be the airport.* I walk down the steps and on to the tarmac. My parents and my sisters are behind me.

We all pile into a car, and I look around in wonder at this new and exotic landscape. As we drive from the airport, we move through rugged and raw terrain. Tall, stringy bark eucalypts are nestled among coconut palm trees. I watch as vivid green and multicolored birds dart in between trees, and a little bit of excitement stirs within me. I want to explore. *Maybe this won't be so bad.* Eventually, we come into a town, and I see a sign "Alyungula" as buildings and flora merge.

I lean forward.

"Why are the houses on stilts, Dad?" I ask.

"It's for when the wet seasons come. If there's a cyclone or flooding, they will protect the houses, and it means the crocs can't swim into the houses either," he says with a slight laugh.

Crocodiles! I shudder.

"What do we do if we see a crocodile, Dad?" I ask.

"You want to run as fast as you can in a straight line, and then as quickly as you can, you change direction, and hopefully it'll fall onto its side. You see, they can't change direction quickly when they're on dry land. If you were in water, it would be a different matter. Best thing is just to avoid being chased by one altogether!" he says. "Now there are two types on the island. You've got the freshies and then the big saltwater crocs. The freshwater crocs are small but can still pack a bite, so always check the river and streams. The beach is going to be out of bounds, I'm afraid, especially near the mangroves as that's where the saltwater crocs hang about."

I nod and make a mental note of how to outrun crocs.

AUSTRALIA, NORTHERN TERRITORY, APRIL 1998— AGE TEN

Hands are on me.

I suddenly wake with alarm. I sit up and quickly pat my hands over my chest and my stomach and pull my nightie down over my hips.

I look around a room that isn't my own. No one is there. My heart beats rapidly in my chest. *It must have been a dream.* I lie back down.

A few hours later, I wake up. There's a sicky sensation in my stomach. I get dressed and walk out of my friend Laura's room. I can hear voices coming from the living room as I walk down the hallway.

"Good morning," I say as I open the hallway door and see Laura, her parents, and her brother.

I smile nervously and walk over to the table where Laura is sitting. The dream moves to the front of my mind as does a foreboding feeling that settles in the pit of my stomach.

As I stand by the table, fumbling with an orange, I notice my friend's brother Tim. He is sitting on the floor with no shirt and is only wearing his boxers. His near nakedness stirs an uncomfortable feeling in me. I look away but not soon enough. As he catches me looking at him, he smiles.

Laura gets up from the table and says, "I'm going to the toilet," and walks out.

Her parents are on the other side of the room as Tim says, "I'm sorry about last night, about coming into the bed. I thought you were my sister." He laughs in a way that makes it sound like he's joking.

I say nothing and stand frozen, staring at him. Thoughts rush in. *He touched me. It was him. What did he do?*

A wave of nausea drags through me. I don't know what to say or do, other than run.

"It's okay," I say quietly. Laura comes back into the room and sits down across from me.

"I don't feel very well. I think I want to go home," I say to her.

She looks a bit sad but goes and tells her parents.

Her parents pass me the telephone and I call home. After a long time, Dad answers. His voice sounds strange as he says, "Hello?"

"It's me. Can you come and get me? I don't feel very well," I whisper.

"I can't right now. I'll have to come a bit later," he says briskly. At his cold reply, the room starts to spin. *I need to get out of here.*

I hang up the phone and turn to Laura's parents.

"I am going to start walking home and meet my dad on the way," I say. My tone implies it's not up for discussion, and I get my bag and leave.

Walking home was not abnormal for me, or any of the children who lived on the island. We were wild, and we all spent most of our time roaming the natural environment around us as though it was our own backyard. I would spend hours out of the house, alone or with friends. I would ride my bike down the quiet streets, lean it against a tall palm tree, and disappear into the lush tropical bushland.

After about thirty minutes, I arrive at the corner of our street. As I walk around, I see our car coming toward me. The car slows to a stop and Dad winds down his window.

"What are you doing?" he asks roughly. I see a pained look on his face, like a man escaping from something.

"I wanted to come home," I say.

"Okay, well, go straight home," he says. I decide not to tell him what happened. I look at my sisters through the back window as he drives off. *Why do they look so upset?* I wonder.

As I near my house, I pause. *The houses look slightly ominous, up on stilts, like they have legs, like the witch, Baba Yaga's.* I walk around the back of the house and up the back steps. I open the back door, and I am greeted with darkness. I look through to the lounge and see all the blinds are down. I hear howling. Nervously, I walk through the kitchen and into the loungeroom.

There, I see my mum crawling around on all fours and howling, "My mum is dead. My mum is dead."

I look at her for a moment and wait for her to notice me, but she doesn't. I quickly walk to my room, close the door, and sit on my bed. The room is lopsided as full force, it all hits me. *Grandma is dead. Tim touched me, and no one at school can know.*

We had been there for about six months before the incident at my friend's house occurred. Coupled with my grandma's passing and my mother's grief, I withdrew into myself. I told no one about what had happened with Tim, but rumors spread. I came to school to find the boys and girls whispering about me. They said I had done things with Tim and I wouldn't leave him alone even though he wasn't interested in being my boyfriend. I didn't know how to speak about what happened, so I became mute. Soon afterward, Laura stopped talking to me and sided with her brother. I became an outsider. But my world wasn't just breaking apart at school. My parents fought, with silence and words, and I got used to seeing food thrown on floors and broken crockery again. I hated being at home, and I hated being at school.

Then one day, I passed my parents' bedroom. Through the slatted window that opened onto the landing I could hear their conversation clearly. I crouched down on the floor below the vent. My dad was pleading with my mum about something. My mum was telling him she didn't love him anymore. I didn't know I could feel any worse, but in that moment, the floor rocked beneath me. She was telling him she wanted to separate. She had met someone else. I bolted back to my room and curled up into a ball on my bed.

My whole world was blowing up around me. There was nowhere for me to get respite and no one to speak to. Even my best friend did not want to be my best friend anymore. She had, earlier that week, handed back the other side of the best friend necklace that hung around my neck. I knew it was because of what had happened with Tim. What else could it have been? My heart ached as anger, sadness, and rage burned inside me.

Within a few months of overhearing the conversation between my parents, my mother left for South Australia, taking two of my younger sisters. My sister Hayley, my father, and I would follow in six weeks.

AUSTRALIA, NORTHERN TERRITORY, SEPTEMBER 1998—AGE ELEVEN

I lie on my bed drawing when my stomach lets out a low rumble. I sit up hungrily and make my way to the kitchen. It's dark and a bit cold as I walk into the living room. I notice my dad's feet hanging over the edge of the couch. *He must be taking a nap.* But then I hear quiet sobs. I walk around and see tears running down his face. I crouch next to him, and his sadness threatens to engulf me as he looks back at me.

Patting his hand, I say, "Think about it, Dad. You don't have to live with Mum anymore."

Later that day, I sit underneath the house near a nest of fire ants that hang from a small bush underneath the metal staircase. I take a small box of matches out of my pocket. One by one, I set them alight, and numbly watch their flammable bottoms create small explosions.

AUSTRALIA, SOUTH AUSTRALIA, OCTOBER 1998—AGE ELEVEN

I look at the pile of boxes and wonder which one contains my stuff. Nothing has been labeled this time. The boxes are stacked high, and I start with a box next to the window. I look outside and see nothing but trees. I open the box and find a cream rectangle-shaped, plastic container, which seems to have no opening. I wonder what it is. I shake it. It's quite heavy and it makes a strange noise, like there's sand in it. I don't know why, but something is strange about it. I know I ought to put it down. I leave the room and walk out to find my mum to ask her what the container is. I see her emptying boxes in the kitchen.

I get closer and ask, "Mum, what's in the cream, rectangle plastic box in the spare room?"

"Grandma's ashes," she replies and looks up at me.

"Oh," I say.

Oh god, I was just shaking my grandma!

We had moved to South Australia because that's where my pop—my mother's dad—lived, along with her cousins and aunty. My father's work changed where he would fly out, working away for two weeks and then coming back to see us for a week. Initially when he came back, he would stay in the house with us. I held out hope for some time that my parents would get back together. That things would be "normal" again. I wanted my father to be around and for both of them to be in the same place. Sometimes they slept in the same bed. I saw that as a sign that things were improving, but nothing ever came of it. I felt equal parts resistance and attachment toward my mother. I was so angry at her for leaving my father, and for being with someone else. I also didn't understand why my father didn't just "do something" to make my mother want to be with him again.

I zoned in on every move my mother made. I didn't like the new friends she made, as it seemed like there was always a party, either in our house or someone else's. As an eleven-year-old, I became sensitive to her anger and shouting, and I found myself taking charge of my sisters so she wouldn't get angry or frustrated. Time management went out the window as did routine. She was often late to pick me up from school or wouldn't wake up in time to get us to school. I started to control what I could but also railed at the lack of control I had.

I also watched as my father become a hollow shell. He lost an immense amount of weight and would sleep much of the time when he came home with us. In the space of a year, it was as though I had completely lost my parents. I felt no line of connection from them to me. I did not talk to them about myself, and they knew nothing of my inner world.

Inside I was screaming. I would run away from home, sometimes disappearing for hours at a time, but I would eventually give in and come home. To my immense anger, my mother hadn't even noticed I had gone, or at least she never said anything. Whenever my emotions would threaten to engulf me, I would stand in the pantry and eat whatever was available until my stomach was tight, removing myself from the heaviness of the insecurity and displacement that crushed me.

This time, I felt no excitement toward starting a new school. After what had happened with my parents, my grandma, Tim, and my friends turning away from me at my last school, I had lost all confidence. When I started at the local school, I made two friends quite soon, but within months of being welcomed into their friendship group, their behavior toward me flipped. From being ignored by them, teased, and openly whispered about when I was within earshot, I started spending my lunchtimes and recesses in the bathroom crying, as the horror of not having any friends on the school yard was intolerable. They told me I was too different, too weird. I didn't know what I had done or how I was being weird. I believed it was because my parents were separated, and that further fueled my anxiety at my perception of coming from a broken home.

I coped with the isolation by sneaking little items in—treasures from home that I would hold on to during lessons and breaks. I would close my eyes and press my fists against my eyelids with the item encased within my palms until I saw stars and completely left my body. As an adult, I learned this is called disassociation. I became very adept at leaving my body in moments of great pain and distress. I adapted quickly, morphing into whomever I needed to be to be accepted and to survive. But as always, the "quiet voice" in between the chaos came forward and made itself known.

I had been thrown into the fire of initiation, and I emerged, no longer a child, but a maiden.

CHAPTER 5

Maidenhood

I sit with her
Under dappled sunlight
I hold her close
And ask "What do you want"

"To be loved" she whispers back

"Oh, my darling, you are love"

We commonly see the maiden archetype being represented as a "damsel in distress," but when a maiden is in her full embodiment, she can be powerful and creative. She is vulnerable yet resilient. Menarche—the first period—marks the beginning of maidenhood. This initiation is an important rite of passage and sets the tone for how a young woman will go on to experience womanhood and possibly motherhood. How the parents of a young girl entering menarche react will have a great effect on the relationship she has with her body, sex, and how she feels about her period. Menarche is the beginning of the life/death/life cycles that occur within a woman's body. When connected to her cycle, a young woman will have the opportunity to cultivate her inner knowing, to learn when to create and when to destroy. Maidenhood is a time of exploration and of a deepening and sharpening of the connection to her inner voice.

WALES, MAY 2020—AGE THIRTY-TWO

"But why is it that when I wasn't with her, I would feel so awful? I would cry and feel sick if I had to wait for her to pick me up or if she went away. I only ever wanted to be with her, or at least up until I met my first boyfriend. Then I didn't miss her or want her as much. I went from not being able to be away from her to not wanting to be around her at all," I told Liz.

"You would have developed an insecure attachment to her. It's not uncommon for this to happen. She was your mother, so of course you wanted to be with her. And when you weren't with her, your body experienced a withdrawal of sorts. You were likely very enmeshed in your relationship with her at that point," Liz responded gently over the phone.

AUSTRALIA, SOUTH AUSTRALIA, SEPTEMBER 2000— AGE THIRTEEN

Pain distracts me from where we are going, and my attention is drawn to the twinge in my belly. My lower back burns, and I press back into the seat to ease the growing ache. I glance over at Mum. She is focused on the road ahead. I wonder what my dad and sisters are doing and hope this weekend isn't completely awful as I've chosen to stay with Mum and Todd, Mum's boyfriend. I hate Todd. He makes my skin crawl, and I don't think he makes my mum all that happy. I've noticed the way he speaks to her with a coldness. I hear her sobs in the middle of the night when she thinks no one is listening because I'm normally awake. I'm scared of dark, ghosts, and of the nightmares that come for me.

I come with her because I cannot stand being away from her, and being with her eases the physical ache and sickness that assails me whenever she is away. I also come because I need to make sure nothing bad happens to her.

The pain in my belly continues. The car slows, and I notice we are in a town now. It's a typical outback town with farmhouses, windmills, and dry sheep pastures. Hills are scattered around. Nothing special. Mum always goes on about how beautiful it is and how it would be nice to live here. I don't want to move again, and anytime she mentions it, I heavily resist the idea.

As we pull up on his drive, a large stone farmhouse greets us. I get out of the car, unsure of where to go. Todd comes out to greet us. I smile nicely but secretly wish he didn't exist. I walk behind them as he shows us into the house. It's cold in the way that these farmhouses hold no heat—cold in the summer, freezing in the winter. I shiver. *It's haunted,* I think.

We walk into the kitchen. Mum and Todd are talking, but I interrupt them. My belly is really hurting now.

"Where's the bathroom?" I ask as I sense something warm on the inside of my legs.

Mum walks me down the corridor and shows me the bathroom. I walk into a large, dark, and earth-smelling room. I hear Mum walk back down the hallway, and I close the door.

I sit down on the toilet seat and pull down my jeans. I am greeted with blood, which is soaking through my knickers and smeared all over the inside of my thighs. I sit there, staring down. *But I only just turned thirteen. This moment is meant to be special. Why here?* Eventually, I call out, "Mum!"

Later that night, I lie on the couch holding my belly as I listen to their voices in the next room. A wave of nausea comes over me. It's mixed with fear. The room is cold. The walls are made of red brick. A seventies lampshade hangs in the center of the room, creating oddly shaped patterns on the walls and floor. I can't fall asleep because I am scared. I am waiting for the ghosts to come. To glide out of the old walls. To descend from the ceiling as I lie sleeping.

I sit up on the couch and wrap the blanket around my shoulders. I want Mum to come out and be with me, but she doesn't. Eventually their voices stop. Hours pass and panic arises. I begin to cry. I am so tired, but I am also so scared. I get up and look out the window. The sky is pitch black, and the stars wink back at me. I can see down to a main road, which gives me some comfort as I watch the occasional car drive by.

I eventually lie back down on the couch. The light is beginning to sting my eyes. I close them and try to still the fear. If a ghost comes out now, what will I do? There's no rationale. I sit up again. And then, the sound. The gentle song from a bird. I look out the window and see the first glimmer of light peeking over the horizon.

Relief washes over me. I survived the night. I lie back down on the couch and listen to the sound of the birds and fall into a deep sleep.

From the moment my parents separated in 1998, I lived in a near state of constant panic. It eased a little when I left home at nineteen, but for the most part, existing in fight or flight was a normal baseline for me. As a young woman, control became my mantra. If I could control every aspect of my life, I would be okay, but I berated myself at how miserably I failed. Panic attacks became a regular thing from the age of fourteen although I did not know at the time what they were. I hid them as well as I could because I didn't want people to think anything was wrong with me. That and they scared me.

Between the age of twelve and seventeen we—my mother, my sisters, and I—moved houses eight times, and this regular upheaval increased my desperate grip on stability. As I blossomed from child to maiden, I discovered a newfound relief from my emotional pain, which came in the form of romantic love. When I first received the affections of a boy, it was a drug like no other. It eased the intensity of worry and pining I experienced whenever I wasn't with my mum. I met my first boyfriend, Jesse, at a party not long after I turned thirteen. I instantly fell in love with him, dissolving the moment we kissed as a new part of myself came online.

AUSTRALIA, SOUTH AUSTRALIA, 2000—AGE THIRTEEN
I walk with Jesse down the hallway. The party we have both been at for the past few hours has come to an end. I'm staying the night, but he's being picked up by his dad. We reach the door, and he turns to hug me. He is a little bit taller than me with dark brown hair that hangs around his eyes. His eyes are dark brown, framed by long thick lashes. He smiles, and I smile back, loving the gap in between his front teeth. He pulls me close, and we hug for a moment. "Goodbye," we both say at the same time, and I turn to walk away.

An urge hits me halfway down the hall, so I stop and turn around. "Jesse," I say, and he steps back into the door frame. I run up to him, rise onto my tiptoes, place my hand on his chest and kiss him gently. His body molds against mine, and in that moment, I am completely whole. He smells like mints and cigarettes, and it's the best smell in the whole world. We both part and smile foolishly at one another.

For days after that night, I couldn't eat and couldn't sleep. I lived and breathed him. He was my first everything, and I'll always have a special place in my heart for him. As a young woman entering maidenhood, the enormity of what I felt for him and the lack of control drove me to distraction. I couldn't stand being away from him, but when I was with him, I no longer knew myself. After two years of being together, we broke up, the relationship ending because I began to feel like a snake writhing, desperate to shed its skin. I didn't know how to be interdependent with someone. It was all or nothing.

Like a pendulum, I swung between extreme emotional states. Some moments, as a teenager, I would relax into myself and into joy, but then I would be assaulted by intrusive thoughts and fear. I put all my painful feelings down to something being wrong with me or other people. My perception of myself was completely dependent on how much attention and love other people gave me.

In any situation when I knew I had to meet new people or put myself out there, I was overcome with excruciating anxiety. But I also longed to be in new, exciting, or different situations. My life was a jumble of extremes. When my mother drank, when we went somewhere, or if my mother went somewhere without me, I would be on edge. She would accuse me of being "no fun" or "too serious" when I begged her not to drink or asked to go home if we had been out at a party for too long. All I kept thinking was I could not wait to move out of my home.

AUSTRALIA, SOUTH AUSTRALIA, 2002—AGE FIFTEEN
I stand in the middle of my new bedroom and sigh as I look around. Unpacked bags and boxes are scattered on the floor. My cat Elki walks in and pushes his head against the back of my legs. My sisters fight loudly in the other room.

I look out the window and see my mum unloading the car.

"Samala, can you help me?" she calls.

I bend down to scratch Elki behind the ears, walk out of the room, and shut the door behind me. In the hallway, I'm greeted by my mum's dog. She is a kelpie-cross border collie.

Always the shadow, she is never far from my mum, who is balancing bags and boxes through the front door.

My two youngest sisters run up the hallway squealing.

"Don't run!" my mum yells.

"Where's Una?" I ask.

"I don't know," my mum says, sounding flustered.

I walk away from my mum to find Una lying on her unmade bed and ask, "What are you doing?"

"Nothing," she says, keeping her eyes down.

She looks sad. I ask, "What's wrong?"

"I don't want to move again. I liked our last house. This house is stupid," she says and bumps her head down intentionally on her forearms.

I stay, hovering by the door. I don't know what to do, and I feel uncomfortable. *I don't want to move either*, I muse, but I don't say that.

"It'll be alright. You'll see," I say and walk back out to my mum, who is carrying more boxes and bags.

"Here, Mum. I'll do that. You go and make yourself a cup of tea." I take the bags and boxes from her and place them in the living room.

Then I round my sisters up and ask, "Who wants to play a game" with my best fake smile as I hear the door to my mum's room close.

As I teen, I spent most of my time at my boyfriend's or, when I did have them, friends' houses. I even made sure I went on the pill without any guidance from my parents. I did my best to be well-behaved. I looked after my sisters, helped clean the house and support my mum by reminding her to buy food and pay the bills, and did my best to problem solve the challenges she faced. But as I progressed through my teenage years, the resentment built. I longed to break free. The guilt I experienced toward my sisters wasn't enough to keep me home because while I saw myself as abandoning them, I had to get away.

We continued to see my father every two weeks and would go and stay with him for a weekend or maybe a week when he was home. For those few days, I would soften a little, but I never brought anyone back to my house. I did not want anyone to see what my home was like. Even I did not want to see the truth. I never said anything to anyone about the anxiety or my worries. I existed like a ghost.

As I moved through puberty, the obsession with my body and how it looked grew. I would stare longingly at the images of the girls in the teenage magazines and wish I looked like them because surely then I would finally be enough. Alone in my room, I would stare at my body in the mirror, extending my desire for control to how I looked, but it was never good enough. I was too short. My boobs were too big, tummy not toned enough. I was too curvy. I became body conscious, and while I wanted attention and validation, I recoiled at the double-edged sword of the never-ending chase for perfection.

After my experience of being bullied again at the new primary school, my parents moved me to a different school. I spent the end of year seven as well as eight and nine at Marbury school. It was an independent private school located in the Adelaide Hills. The school itself was situated in a heritage listed home and garden, which was built in 1888, and the high school part of the school was in "Wairoa House." As the students of Marbury, we roamed the stunning gardens that surrounded the manor house. We would take our lunch in the grotto, sit among the camelia trees or lie out on the large lawns during the summer. It was a truly magical place to learn, and that learning style had suited me the most. We called the teachers by their first names, and it was a coeducational, independent, noncompetitive, and nonauthoritarian school. There, I met Jesse and was welcoming of friends.

But as year ten loomed, the tone and feel to Marbury changed. I asked to move to an all-girls school for the rest of high school because of its extensive dance, drama, and music classes as thoughts of the future were grabbing my attention. But at the beginning of year ten, the anxiety was at its all-time highest. My mother had bought a house not long after I started at the new school, and I experienced daily dread around the bills remaining unpaid and feared moving again. I lasted four weeks in the new school and begged to be taken out as my anxiety and inability to make new friends sent me into a daily tailspin.

I spent the rest year ten remote learning by myself. I stayed at home and learned over telephone conference calls, but I rarely went into those calls. Most of that year was compiled with reading, going on long walks, and listening to Tori Amos. I spent the majority of year ten alone. Somewhere in my relationship with Jesse, I had lost all my friends from Marbury. When Jesse and I broke up just after I turned fifteen, I found myself alone.

But in that aloneness, something in me awoke and a maturity unfolded. I started doing yoga, connecting with the moon and my menstrual cycle. A sense of connection to something else emerged as well. My concern over my body lessened as I developed a different relationship with it. I became interested in self-improvement, health, and well-being. I read books like *The Power of Compassion* by the Dalai Lama to learn how to love myself more. I was deeply affected by a book called *Opening the Lotus: A Woman's Guide to Buddhism* written by Sandy Boucher.

Toward the end of that year, I felt the same urge for change, a calling within. I couldn't explain it, but I just knew I needed to go to school. I experienced these god moments—as I call them—a lot throughout my life. I knew I needed to make the next move. I wanted to make friends and desired another chance to open myself up, but I refused to go to the local high school. I knew from seeing the students who went there that I wouldn't survive, let alone fit in. The only other option was a private Lutheran high school. Hope stirred within me, and despite my home life being chaotic, I was excited for the chance of something new.

AUSTRALIA, SOUTH AUSTRALIA, 2003—AGE FIFTEEN

I stand in a busy corridor. Students walk past me, glancing at me for a moment and then walking on. My school bag is heavy on my back. I adjust my skirt, ensuring it's the correct length and push any free strands of hair off my face. My palms are sweaty and my face tingles. The drive to run hits me. *This is a* huge *mistake*. But then I see a girl walking toward me. She has long dark hair and big brown eyes.

She smiles as she walks up to me. "Hi, I'm Danielle," she says, with full confidence.

Relief washes over me. *I'm saved.*

"I'm Samala," I say.

"You must be new."

"I am, and I'm a bit lost. I need to get to biology," I say.

"I'll show you where to go," she says, and we walk together.

As she guides me, she points to various classrooms and people. My heartbeat slows and the desire to run eases. *I hope she becomes my friend, she's nice.*

Later that day, I walk out of the year eleven locker corridor and into the courtyard. I'm balancing a huge stack of textbooks in my arms. Over the top of the books, I notice an intimidatingly large group of boys gathered a few meters ahead of me. *Oh no!*

I'm very aware that I am new and must walk past them. As I near them, their laughter stops for a moment, and as I walk in front of them, I trip. All my books tumble forward onto the floor. My face burns as I kneel and frantically gather them into my arms. *Floor, please swallow me.* Then I hear one of the boys say, "Want some help with that?" *and I cringe as they all erupt with raucous laughter.*

As it turns out, that boy was Nicholas. Who later that year would become my boyfriend.

During year eleven, just as I had dreaded, my mother ended up having to sell the house and we moved again. But I weathered this, as I had developed solid friendships with Danielle and Amber—who I met a little later after Danielle. We became incredibly close, and while I was met with challenges from my home life, these relationships kept me afloat. My friends never said anything about the fact that I never asked them over. And I didn't tell them what was going on at home because, in truth, I didn't know what to say. I did my best to keep my home life and my school life separate.

Just after my sixteenth birthday, Nicholas and I started dating. I juggled my new friendships, as they were so important to me, and my relationship with him. I juggled my anxiety, my fears, and my hopes. I kept my head above water and did my best to look after everyone.

But I would often feel bereft, as bad things kept happening, no matter how hard I tried to stop them.

AUSTRALIA, SOUTH AUSTRALIA, 2003—AGE SIXTEEN

We're in another new house. I wake up before everyone else. My sisters and Mum are still asleep. I can smell cat poo, but I can't find it. I can also smell cat pee. It's coming from the pile of unwashed clothes in the laundry. I walk to the kitchen and open the cupboard, but no food is there. I open the fridge. I find a little milk and butter. I scrape mold off the bread and make some toast.

I feel the overwhelming urge to scream and cry, but I don't. Instead, I stuff as much toast down as possible while leaving enough for my sisters. I place my hand on my belly and pull at the skin underneath my checkered navy blue and maroon school dress.

I hunt around the house for change so I can buy some lunch at school. I find some spare fifty-cent pieces. Half an hour later, everyone is still asleep. I start to panic, afraid I'm going to miss the bus.

I walk into Mum's room, which is dark and heavy. I can't see her as she is buried under covers and pillows. I peel back the covers and see that her hair is covering her face.

I reach out to touch her shoulder. "Mum," I say in a whisper. "Mum, can you wake up? We'll be late for school." Then I go and wake the girls up.

Then follows an hour of screaming as they don't want to go to school, and there's no food.

"Well, I'm just a terrible mother. Aren't I! A real shit mother. Why don't you all go and get another mother. Maybe one of your dad's perfect girlfriends?" I hear Mum yell from the other room.

My chest feels tight. I'm going to be late. I just want to get to school.

"Mum, we need to go. I'm going to be late," I say with a tight chest as I walk into the room where my sisters and Mum are.

Finally, we all pile into the car.

"Bugger," Mum says. "The car is nearly out of gas."

I groan audibly as I look over at the flashing red fuel light, and my stomach twists into a knot. *Why does she never put gas in the car? Why does she never buy food? Why does she always leave everything to the last minute?*

My sisters begin to fight until every time we go down a hill, Mum puts the car in neutral and we all lean forward to push the car along. I look at my youngest sister as she laughs when we do this. I laugh nervously alongside her. We coast into the gas station. Five dollars in the car.

And I know we'll do it all again tomorrow.

AUSTRALIA, SOUTH AUSTRALIA, EARLY 2004—AGE SIXTEEN

I stand in my mum's bedroom holding a small kitchen knife. She's sitting on the bed opposite me as I wave the knife in the air frantically over my head.

"I can't *take it anymore*! I don't want to live here. I would rather kill myself right now than go on like this!" Tears stream down my face as my body explodes with anger and rage.

My two younger sisters are hiding in the other room. Una is on the bed by my mum, crying.

"I can't stand the fighting. I can't stand the mess. I hate being so far away from my friends. Constantly worrying about getting to school on time. I want to live with Dad. Call Dad now," I scream.

Mum has a look of fear on her face. I am slightly taller and stronger than her now. My teenage rage is just as powerful as hers. She takes out her phone and calls my dad.

I hear him answer and Mum says, "Talk to your daughter," and holds out the phone for me.

I walk forward, take the phone, and walk out of the room.

"Dad," I cry. "Dad, I can't live here anymore. It's too stressful. I want to be with you. I want to be closer to school and my friends. I need to live with you. I will walk to school myself.

I'll get my own food. I just can't be here anymore. I'm begging you," I say.

After a few minutes, I walk back in the room. "Dad says I can live with him." I hand her the phone.

My father accepted that my reason for wanting to move in with him was the desire to be closer to school and my friends. He knew things were hard with my mother, but I couldn't be completely honest because I felt guilty and ashamed. I didn't want people to think badly of my mother, and I didn't want people to think badly of my sisters. I didn't want people to think badly of me. I just wanted the chaos to end. I needed peace and the solution that came to me was me no longer being at home with my mother and my sisters.

Year twelve began with me moving into my father's house, which was a forty-five-minute walk from my school. I relished the newfound independence and joyously walked back and forth every day. I would walk to school with my bag on front ways, with the latest Harry Potter book resting on top. I would get to school early, make my own lunches, clean the house, and buy my own food. My father came home every two weeks, and I would see my sisters during that time, but I was essentially living by myself. For the first time, I had my own space, and it was of the most value to me.

But the peace was interrupted by the nagging feeling, and I would be caught off guard as listlessness came over me. Familiar habits such as lying on my bed thinking about all the bad things that could happen returned. Despite my efforts to create a boundary between me and stress, I would arrive home from school and find my mother's car parked in the driveway and her inside the house. "We've come to stay with you," she would say. A lump would swell in my throat. I knew it meant she had no food. I worried for my sisters terribly, but I couldn't do anything. I missed them, but I was somehow able to cut those feelings off.

I concentrated on my friends, boyfriend, and school. I fell into the safety of my relationship with Nicholas. He was sweet, loving, and supportive. Sometimes his level of adoration irritated me, and within a year or so of our relationship, I started to feel unsettled. A restlessness flooded my body. I had the urge to move, to change, and to be somewhere different. My father was now working in Western Australia again, and although I had lived in multiple places in Australia, Western Australia had always been my home place, and it was my birthplace.

Not long after I finished year twelve, I traveled to Perth to stay with my father. The instant I landed and got off the plane, "home" echoed in my body. I spent the week catching the bus to the beach, visiting the Fremantle Markets, and frequenting cute cafés. I had such fond memories of Perth; of the times I had spent with my nanna in Fremantle or my cousins when I was younger. Perth was home to me. It had an energy that drew me to it, and I knew I had to leave Adelaide.

When I returned to Adelaide, I told Nicholas I wanted to move to Perth. I noticed a part of me that maybe wanted to go alone, but I wasn't brave enough to be honest. I avoided confronting those feelings, and together, we made the necessary plans to move over. In May 2006, just before I turned nineteen, Nicholas and I moved all our belongings into a tiny flat in North Perth. We had both secured jobs, and it was our first rental. It was also the first time we had lived with anyone but our families. Despite any worries, at that moment in time, I was so proud of us.

We had transformed into adults.

CHAPTER 6

Soul Skin

Take it,
My soul
I don't need it,
For you will be my soul now

When I read the myth of the selkie bride who married a human and gave up her seal skin, I began to see the ways in which I had given up parts of myself to be loved by others. Over time, like the woman without her seal skin, I began to wither and dry. Unlike the selkie, I gave my seal skin away a few times before I learned the important lesson of holding on to and nurturing my wild nature.

WESTERN AUSTRALIA, LATE MAY 2006—AGE EIGHTEEN
I walk toward a café situated in a suburb just outside of Perth city center. As I approach the entrance, I pause to look around. It's early morning, and the sun shines through the large concertina doors that line the front of the building. I look down at my phone to see a text from Nicholas.

Nicholas: Good luck. luv u xx

Me: u 2 xx

I tuck my phone into my backpack and breathe in audibly followed by a big exhale.

I walk forward to a large counter where a girl stands behind it. She smiles and says, "Hi, how are you doing? What can I get for you today?"

I quickly reply, "Oh I'm new. As in, I'm starting a job here today."

"Oh no worries. Give me a minute and I'll be right back." She walks away, and I step back from the counter.

As I step back, I notice a man standing behind the coffee machine. He looks over at me, and for an instant our eyes meet. A flash of a thought: *He's for you.* I look away and dismiss that strange intrusion.

But I can't help but notice the tingly sensation in my body.

WALES, JULY 2020—AGE THIRTY-TWO
I sat in the driver's seat of my parked car outside my house. Liz was silent on the other end of the phone while I spoke.

"I just wonder why, why I kept entering relationships. Why I did the things I did. Especially with Simon. I knew it wasn't right, I knew deep down but I still moved. I don't regret it, but

I just wonder why. Was it because I was running away from my family? It's like when I meet someone, I completely lose myself, and then I wake up years later in that relationship wondering how the hell I got there."

AUSTRALIA, JUNE 2006—AGE EIGHTEEN
"It's been almost six months since we had sex," Nicholas says, lying next to me in our bed.

I lie on my back, thinking about how this whole conversation is creating a well of discomfort and resistance in my body.

"I know. I just don't feel like it. It's not you. It's just me. I really love you. I just need some space," I say.

"It seems like it's more than that. The last time we had sex was New Year's Day. I even wrote it down. Things have been different since we moved here. You're different. Distant. Do you still want to be with me?"

I almost hear a plea in his voice as he speaks, and a wave of guilt and disgust toward myself hits me. Why can't I just say I don't know how I feel? Why can't I say I don't know what I want anymore? Why can't I say I spend my days off work wandering around Perth like a lost child who doesn't know who she is?

"It's like, we used to have so much in common. I used to know what you liked, what you were into, and now I don't know that I know you at all anymore," he says and rolls over away from me. I stare up at the ceiling. I don't have an answer for him because I don't know either.

It wasn't lost on me, the similarity between my feelings toward Jesse and then Nicholas as the end of our relationship was clearly looming. That how once the initial rush of a new relationship wore off, I became hollow and distant. At the beginning, I morphed into a version of me that I perceived suited them. But then, two or three years later, I would meet a part of myself in the bathroom or on a long walk, normally when I was alone, and she would come at me, angry, saying, "What are you doing? Why are you pretending to be someone you're not?" But the trouble was, when I *was* myself, another part of me would step in and say, "Best not to do that. Being yourself is risky." I was confused and remained confused for quite some time.

What I would learn, years later of course, was that I had an anxious-avoidant attachment style. This type of attachment style meant I would attach very quickly to someone I had "feelings" for, and even if there were plenty of red flags, they were practically invisible to me. So when Nicholas began to want more from me, my avoidant style was activated. This ability to shut down and turn off emotions was helpful as a young child, but it meant I could go from being wildly in "love" with someone and within moments shut down all feelings if needed. Of course, at this point and up until my early thirties, I had no idea this dynamic was playing out among everything else.

As August 2006 approached, Nicholas and I had become ghosts in the shell of our relationship. The man who had been standing behind the coffee machine on that first day of work—whose name was Simon—did not help my distance. He had quickly become a close work friend and within a few months of working together, Simon and I developed a close bond. I was in awe of his worldliness, his intellect, and his wide passionate taste in music. We would talk for hours about movies and music. While I became numb to the relationship that was disintegrating with Nicholas, I attached to Simon.

At first, I told myself we were just good friends and things between Nicholas and me would get better. But eventually, as my nineteenth birthday passed, I knew I couldn't waste anymore of Nicholas's time. I hated that he was hurting, and I had to admit to myself that my feelings toward Simon were more than "friendship" ones. It was as quick as "I don't love you anymore" and the relationship between Nicholas and me was severed. I closed myself off to Nicholas's pain, and there was no more to be said. I turned cold, cutting myself off from everything I was feeling.

And as quickly as we had moved into our flat, we moved out. We took our things, and I moved in with my father just north of Perth City while Nicholas moved south. He stayed in Perth for a little while longer but eventually went back to South Australia. Nicholas handled the ending of our relationship with such grace and courage. In the months afterward, we parted ways in friendship.

SAMALA'S JOURNAL, NOVEMBER 2006—AGE NINETEEN
"Am I okay?"
I'll ask myself over and over
Am I alright?
And I'll stare at my reflection hoping for an answer
Who is this person that becomes me?
Who robs me, who takes me and why does she come with no warning, no hello, she just takes over and it brings tears to my eyes.
Big heavy warm tears that slide like rain down my cheeks, soaking my lips in salt.
She, licks them off and spits them out like darts.
She.
She takes all and I am dead with the aftermath.
The aftermath of me.

Simon and I started seeing each other a few months after the relationship between Nicholas and me ended. But it was not smooth sailing. Our relationship had a different tone, and I began to feel anxious and unsure of myself. Simon had moved from the UK with an ex-partner. Between that ending and Simon and me beginning to see each other, at times Simon wasn't sure what he wanted. We moved back and forth between being "on and off" for six months. In which time, I drove myself to distraction. My mental health plummeted to the point where I couldn't eat, and some days I couldn't leave the house. All I could think about was how much I wanted to be with Simon, and if we didn't end up together, I would surely die.

I became an expert at reading his emotions and became hypervigilant to his moods. I did everything to make myself as desirable as possible, and I did my best to contain my emotional outbursts. At one point, I went to a doctor to ask for help. I was told I had anxiety and was prescribed antidepressants, but I didn't take them. I refused to take them because my perception at the time was "I didn't want to be like my mum." I was filled with self-loathing and criticized myself for not being able to "snap" out of it. The only thing that would stop the immense pain was when Simon was loving or did something to show love. Then, the anxiety and "madness" would dissipate.

Eventually, we did "get together" officially, and once again, I disappeared into that relationship. I took on all his likes, dislikes, and dimmed my light. He, of course, never asked me to do that, but I simply did not know how to be my fullest self with anyone. Even though we were together, I still experienced anxiety within the relationship. Whenever we had an argument, or even the slightest hint of conflict, I would fret and pine, believing he would leave me.

During one of our arguments, I was crying inconsolably, so much so that he left the room. I sat on the bed and scratched my arms until they were red raw as the sheer panic of being left and ignored turned me inside out. I thought I was crazy, and at times he would verbally echo that back to me. I had no idea how to communicate my needs, and we both existed in a volatile dynamic of push and pull.

Whenever I was by myself, intrusive thoughts would slide in. Such as "he doesn't really love you" or "he's going to leave you." I never truly questioned whether I was happy with the relationship. I was consumed by whether *he* loved me and argued with myself about whether he was going abandon me or not. I was currently unaware of my deep fear of abandonment or any of my other wounds. I would read his moods, his energy, and ask him, "What's wrong?" He would say nothing, but I would persist until it ended in an argument.

I could focus on little else apart from our relationship. I would still have days when I struggled to get to work or socialize. I was exhausted a lot of the time. At times, we had an unbalanced dynamic between us. I believed he saw me as young and immature, due to our eight-year age difference, and I projected a lot of my insecurities on to him, and of course vice versa. We did not communicate well, and I know on my part I could never be completely honest because of my fear of his reaction. This meant I would often retract my truth, changing it or altering it in order to fit his needs. Over time, I harbored resentment, which I did not acknowledge until years after our relationship ended.

I never thought too much about the future. I told myself I was happy to just have him for the moment. I lived by his terms, what he wanted for the relationship, and what he envisioned as a future for us. I allowed myself to be pushed, and he had no other way of knowing it wasn't always what I wanted because I never said anything otherwise, to myself or to anyone.

In August 2007, when Simon returned from visiting Wales and said to me, "I want to go home," there was never a question that I would follow.

CHAPTER 7

Running

So, I ran
Across the world
Searching for a way to close
The open wounds
Looking to heal you in every space
I could not be close enough
But then I could not be far enough
When you left, I would cry
When you came back, I would hide
But the one day
I realized that I could not heal you
It was never in my power to fix you
And that the only one I ever needed to heal
To remember
To love
Was me

SAMALA'S JOURNAL—JULY 2020
"I have these moments where I feel like my body is spinning. About to explode. There is so much guilt, and so much shame. For all that I have done. I am so angry at myself."

AUSTRALIA, WESTERN AUSTRALIA, SEPTEMBER 2007
I freeze as Simon says, "I want to move back to the UK."

He's leaving me, I realize. I try my best not to show the panic building inside of me as we sit at the circular table in our kitchen. It's early spring, and the sunlight dapples through the high window behind me making patterns on Simon's face. My automatic response is, "Well, then I'll come with you."

He tells me it's up to me. If I want to come I can, but he is certain he wants to move back to Wales.

WALES, JULY 2020—AGE THIRTY-TWO
"It's not lost on me that when Simon told me he wanted to move back to Wales it was almost the same as when I told my high school boyfriend Nicholas I wanted to move to Perth. It feels karmic and ironic, but I couldn't see it then," I said as I walked along a woodland trail not far from my house.

It was a beautiful, warm, summer day, and sunlight filtered through the large fat green leaves onto the pavement.

"Samala, I think that given your anxious state and attachment style at the time, it would have been nearly impossible for you to say no and not go. Perhaps in time, the answers and reason for your move and everything else will become clearer to you."

"I think that too. I guess I am holding some resentment, perhaps, and guilt over the way things ended. Being separated from the father of my children was never something I wanted. Especially after my own experiences."

AUSTRALIA, WESTERN AUSTRALIA, 2007—AGE TWENTY
After the initial conversation with Simon, the war in my mind instantly began. I had no other option but to move. Initially, I gave myself no time to think it through. I was going. But then, despite leaving home over three years ago, my mother's well-being and current state was always in the back of my mind. I worried constantly. In between my own anxious states and worrying about my relationship with Simon, I worried about her. Still, at times, she did not have any money or was in emotional turbulence or a depression. Her relationship with Todd had ended somewhere around the time when I was fourteen, and during the time I was contemplating the move to the UK, she was living with a partner.

I knew she wasn't happy, and I closed myself off to a lot of what she was experiencing. Whenever she would call, I would listen to her worries and concerns, and I did my best to problem-solve. After the phone calls, I would tailspin, praying, "Please just let her be okay. Please look after her." My belief was if she could just be safe and stable, so much of the pain, suffering, and worry that existed in me would dissolve. It never occurred to me that it wasn't my responsibility. At this point in my life, I did not think about my childhood or my teenagerhood, but I had an itchy feeling underneath. I knew something wasn't right, but I still couldn't put my finger on it. She was my mother after all, and shouldn't I just accept that's how she was? Surely all mothers were this way.

On reflection, I see now how society normalized dysfunctional familial behavior. "They're family." "That's just how they are."

I never believed I was allowed to set boundaries and negotiate a different way of interacting. I had never even had a conversation about boundaries. I never believed I could say anything.

My mind, just like a fridge, kept the mold safely hidden underneath while it festered. I was also busy finding my worth in a romantic relationship. It was just too painful to see the full truth of what was beneath and face up to the constant exhaustion and worry I wrestled with daily. So, instead I looked for my wholeness in, and distracted myself with, relationships.

A few days after that conversation with Simon, I was sitting on the beach watching the waves lick the shoreline and turning everything over in my mind. I thought about being away from my family and being further away from my mother. I felt a slight tinge of relief at the thought of being further away, but I pushed that aside because guilt immediately jumped out at the thought of me wanting to get as far away as possible. And perhaps I was wanting too.

To this day, I still cannot tell you I had complete clarity in the decision-making process, but nonetheless, a big enough yes moved through me. The *yes* propelled me forward as did the growing desire to get away from the "responsibility" and feelings that would surface whenever I thought about my mother, and my focus stayed solely on the move.

Perhaps it was my attachment to Simon, but all doubts were blocked out. I had made my choice, and despite a few people playing devil's advocate, I did not hear them. I did not entertain any thoughts about what would happen if it didn't work out. I never imagined we would get married or have children, mainly because Simon had said he did not want to get married, and he wasn't all that keen on having children. I was purely in the moment, living and breathing our relationship.

Then followed a year of preparations and sorting out visas. I often had thoughts that maybe we would not move, and sometimes I entertained the idea of not going with him. But something pulled me. Something kept me going with the plans. Perhaps I was always meant to be here.

ENGLAND, HEATHROW AIRPORT, JULY 2008—ALMOST TWENTY-ONE

I pull my new red coat over my shoulders and walk out of Heathrow Airport. Simon gestures me toward a gray Ford Kia. I am exhausted by the long-haul flight, but I am filled with adrenaline and excitement to finally be here. It hasn't fully sunk in that I have just moved countries. Simon and I chat away, and I look around, taking it all in as though I have never *seen* before. Everything is so *different*. Nothing is quite like arriving in a new place for the first time, especially another country. I notice that Simon's accent is stronger. I marvel at the trees; they are so *green* and are practically exploding with leaves and vibrancy.

The sky looks different. It's softer, lower with wispy white clouds scattered here and there. I peer at the sides of the roads, which are covered in fresh, *alive*, foliage—unlike in Western Australia where the sides of the freeway are simply red and brown dirt. It is as though mother nature herself is taking full advantage of every available crevasse. If there's a space, something green will grow. Even the air is filled with white cottony tree pollen, and like fairies, they glide between trees. *I'm only on the M4 at this point, but it's breathtaking.*

But the high of the arrival soon made way for the reality of the situation. We arrived during the recession. There were hardly any jobs. We started off by living with his parents, and my savings bolstered us. The hospitality industry, in which I had been employed in Perth, was nonexistent and not to the same standard. One afternoon, as I walked down the high street of a valley town, the shock of what I had done hit me. Later that day, I wrote a letter to my sister, which I never sent, telling her I had made a huge mistake and wanted to come home.

The homesickness for the land that I had come from assailed me. I missed my family. I missed the familiarity. And something I did not expect was the intense pining for my birth country. Even now, fourteen years later, I miss the land like a severed part of me. There is no place like Oz. But of course, I stayed, and I spoke little of my discontent to Simon. I did not want to displease him, and after all, it was my choice to move here.

I struggled with fitting in. At the time, with the age gap between Simon and me, I was acutely aware that I was "younger." I placed myself on the outside. He had a big family, and I thought I wasn't accepted. I would become anxious at big family gatherings. I never knew who to talk to, and I would feel awkward as I did my best to be a part of the group. Most likely, I came across as aloof. I stood on the outside not knowing how to let people in. It was me rejecting me, but I did not realize this until many years later. His family had been nothing but loving. I simply could not receive that love and welcome. I did not know what to do with a family that loved and cared for each other.

Toward the end of 2008, Simon, his sister, and his parents bought a pub. Simon, his sister, and I moved into the flat above the pub. I don't believe it ever came up in conversation, but it wasn't intended that I would work there. It wasn't an area of the hospitality industry I wanted to work in because I had a very strong aversion to drinking at that point in my life. Instead, I landed a job working in a call center for a bank. I stayed there for three months before I quit.

At that point, I did not know what I wanted to do or what any of my desires were, so I began the search for what I knew, hospitality, and eventually got a job in a café. I bounced around jobs until I landed an assistant manager role for a bakery chain. I felt a momentary relief, but my anxiety returned in new ways. I would clock watch all day. Seeing each hour pass and think it's an hour closer to my death. But I equally longed for the working days to end. I would sit outside on my ten-minute morning break and lose myself in the fresh air and open sky. I would pretend for a moment that I was somewhere else—somewhere warm and sunny.

Slowly, my anxiety creeped in and affected my ability to trust in myself. I assumed if anything went wrong, it was automatically my fault. I was riddled with fears of getting things wrong such as closing the shop wrong or doing the rosters wrong. I lived in fear of answering my phone in case someone was calling to reprimand me. I threw my attention into being a good girlfriend but to no avail. I was assailed with sensations of sadness, ennui, and a listlessness that ran the show.

In the moments when I did fall into complete darkness, if I stayed there long enough, something would emerge. An idea. Some inspiration. And I would perk up for a time. I would draw or go for long walks and that would take the edge off the undertow that was ready to pull me under again. At that point, I did not have any self-knowledge or the tools to create a lasting shift within myself.

I had no idea who I was and believed I required fixing. I was operating through unconscious programming, and my body was geared toward survival. It sought out familiarity, even if that familiarity mirrored the dynamics I had been exposed to and experienced as a child and teen. To create a life on that sort of foundation was only ever going to end in one way. I was building a life on quicksand, and I couldn't sustain what I was creating.

In 2009, Simon and I were at a Christmas party when we met a couple and their newborn baby. I noticed how Simon looked at the baby, and when he suggested that we might plan to have a baby a few days later, I wasn't as shocked as I could have been. But I was still taken aback, mainly because I had never considered he would suggest such a thing. However, my immediate answer was a whole-body *yes* because despite any niggling doubts about how content I was, and whether our relationship was solid, I knew I wanted to get pregnant. I had never been so sure about anything.

ENGLAND, MARCH 2010—AGE TWENTY-TWO

I loosen the tie of my spotted dressing gown and take a sip of tea. I flick through a magazine and look up to see Simon standing against the counter with a glass of wine. Our dog, Jess, which we had bought a few months earlier, is curled up by my feet. I watch as Simon walks over to his phone and changes the music. Nora Jones begins to play. Then he walks over to me, sits down at the table, and takes my hands. The energy in the room shifts, and I know something serious is about to happen. I remain silent as he starts to speak.

"Samala, I want you to know how much I love you. I want you to know just how important you are, and now that we are trying for a baby. I just, I think that it's time for…" He pauses to catch his breath. "I guess what I'm trying to say is will you marry me?" He drops down on his knee next to me. Jess jumps up and licks Simon's face.

It feels like hours pass before I say, "Yes!" Though simultaneously, I sense a quiet *no* within me. I shake it off and push it down, and I fall into the high of it all. *It's finally happening.* Everything I never thought would happen is happening.

Instead of listening to that no, I ignored what I now know is how my intuition speaks to me. It's very quiet. It's very subtle, and it only speaks once, in the moment. It was easy to pretend I never sensed the no and dove into planning a wedding. I ignored the arguments and the tension, staying focused on getting pregnant. Which wasn't happening quickly enough, to which I chastised myself for not being good enough to even get pregnant. But then eventually, the ripple of change reached out, and my inner voice nudged me to take a pregnancy test early one morning in 2010.

I will never forget the feeling of seeing the words "Pregnant one to three weeks."

I held the test for what seemed like a lifetime. The joy that filled my body was indescribable. I placed my hand on my belly and inhaled deeply. I had known, and I marveled at that. I wanted to stay there and revel in this sacred piece of knowledge for a just a while longer. It was just me and my little fish.

Eventually, I woke up Simon to tell him. And of course, he was overjoyed. Our joy was palpable, but soon the mutual joy gave way to darker emotions and the rocky foundations I lived on began to shake—those sharp moments where my body would remind me of a pain felt long ago. When he drank, or went to parties, or stayed out late with friends, even though it was a completely different scenario to what I had experienced as a child, I was triggered and a wall would go up. I would cry, retreat into myself, and do my best to mitigate his emotions.

But my first pregnancy was beautiful, and amid all the sadness that shimmered at the edges of me and the deeply unsettling feelings that assailed me, I anchored my whole self to this baby. Some days, sorrow hit me at the thought of it no longer being in my belly because for the first time in my life I didn't feel alone. And the pure joy and aliveness that I experienced moved through me. I spoke to it, caressed my belly, and played it classical music. I loved it with my whole being. I knew nothing of parenting or what awaited me, but I knew I would love this little baby with my entire heart and soul.

Not long after I became pregnant, I reached the end of my tether with my job at the bakery. One afternoon, when I was by myself, I asked myself, "If you could do anything all day long, what would it be?" and the answer that came was "exercise." I had always loved exercising, dancing, and well-being, albeit a little too much at times.

I enrolled in a personal training diploma, which fortuitously ended up with me landing a job in the gym where I had completed the certification. I'll never forget getting the job or the face of the gym manager six weeks later when I said I'd be going on maternity leave in six months.

On February 21, 2011, at around 8:20 p.m., my son Luke was born. It was a challenging labor, but nothing prepared me for the hours and weeks that would follow as this little baby rocked my world. I instinctively knew what to do, but my people-pleasing nature pushed forward. I allowed myself to be swayed into how I should mother him and ignored my instincts as they screamed at me.

Postpartum, I struggled with my body and my identity. I did not know who I was as a mum, let alone as a fiancée. A fire was burning within me, but I put it out and lost myself in this new role. I felt the cavern grow between Simon and me—the fights, the retreating, the distance, and the way neither of us knew how to come back to one another. It was as though Luke was the only thing holding us together.

I went back to work just before my twenty-fourth birthday. Luke was five months old. Leaving him was gut wrenching. The sheer emotional turmoil I experienced when I would drop him off at his nan's to do a night shift had me in tears the entire way to work. I was torn between wanting to be at home with my son but needing to keep my job. My only way of coping was to close my heart to the pain, and I convinced myself I was happy going back to work. But in truth, I wasn't. I wasn't okay.

I was riddled with anxiety whenever Luke was away from me. It became so bad that if someone else was holding him while I was there, my whole body would scream until he was given back to me. I was convinced everyone wanted to take him away from me. I was terrified of losing him. I grieved him no longer being in my belly for months after he was born. I know now that I had postpartum depression and anxiety, which was only amplified by the unhealed complex trauma and attachment issues raging inside of me. On the outside, I put on a brave face because the last thing I wanted was for people to think I was crazy, presume I was an unfit mother, and take him from me.

As time went on and the wedding plans became "cemented," a different kind of anxiety began to build in me. Simon and I weren't connecting. My body was closed off to him, and I knew it hurt him. I had no idea how to communicate what I was feeling. I feared the emotions he showed when he was hurt. All I kept thinking was that I was Rose from *Titanic*, with no control over her life, standing in the middle of the room screaming. And no one looked up. No one saw me.

So, I ran toward the edge of the ship and jumped off into the cold water and upended my life.

I had been on the phone with my father early in December 2011, and I said I was having second thoughts about getting married. After I finished the phone call, I knew with certainty that I had to call off the engagement. I needed at least that much to stop. I told Simon I couldn't marry him. The heartache and pain that erupted from him floored me. We made an appointment to see a counselor. But when we went, we couldn't find anything to work on. He was angry and hurt. And I had shut myself off to both his and my feelings. The more he clung to me, the more I pulled away.

By February 2012, we were living separately. After Simon and I separated, I fell into a deep depression. The year began in a complete blur. I was merely surviving. Despite that initial drive to leave, I was now swimming in a sea of guilt and grief. I had done the thing I had never wanted to do. I had ripped apart our lives. I was away from my one-year-old baby for half the week. I had no family. I isolated myself and pushed everyone away. I may as well have been driftwood at sea.

I managed to keep my job, looked after my beautiful son, and kept up a brave face to those I did see. But I struggled to keep meaningful connections and plummeted into a dark space. I became another version of myself. I was in a depression and the thread that connected me to life was temporarily severed. I saw myself as empty. Broken. A failure. I would sleep, eat, and dissolve into binge watching Netflix when my son was not with me. I would lie on his bed when he wasn't there and cry or watch the TV shows he loved for comfort. I would hug his soft toys and refold his clothes.

I became addicted to exercising. My mind raced and my heart pounded daily. And into the darkness, before I fell asleep, I would whisper, "Save me, please. Someone save me." I never thought the answer to all my heartache and pain started and ended with me.

I could not see that I was running from myself.

CHAPTER 8

The Choice

―

Winding, winding
Down a path
Who will you choose?
Yourself,
Or him

WALES, MAY 2015—AGE TWENTY-SEVEN

I drop to the floor as my entire body reacts to what has just happened. I curl forward moving into a lopsided child's pose, attempting to keep my body from breaking into millions of shards. My forehead touches the floor as fat tears soak my face and cascade downward. I wrap my arms around belly. I notice that it is rounder and cry out audibly, "He's left me. I can't believe he left me. God, please tell me what to do. Please, I need someone to tell me what to do."

WALES, FEBRUARY 2013—AGE TWENTY-FIVE

After a year of navigating a new coparenting relationship with Simon and living by myself, I came to the realization that I had to do something about my mental state of being. When I surveyed my current circumstances, I was a single mother with no family support outside of Simon and the support his parents offered. I had none of my own family nearby. For the first time, I wished I had my family near me.

I struggled financially, and my emotions were turbulent, going from black depressions to moments of high anxiety. I didn't socialize, and I found it almost impossible to leave my flat and go anywhere new. I always ensured that Luke had what he needed, and I managed to keep myself on an even keel when he was with me, but I wanted to give him more. I wanted to give him more of me. Some days, I would look at the bills on the counter and despair, wondering how I would survive.

I would stand frozen for hours, fretting in attempt to problem-solve my life. I lived from breath to breath, often going to bed when Luke did at 6 p.m. just to escape the emotions that flooded me as the sadness and hopelessness that consumed me was dulled when I slept. Despite knowing that the relationship between Simon and me needed to end, I was spinning in the chaos and guilt. At the time, I could not see the deeper layers of pain and trauma that existed beneath me, only the desire to run and escape the same wounds, which were just in a different form.

I decided I needed to get help, and I went to the doctor, explaining how I was feeling. The doctor said I had postpartum depression, which was common. He gave me a prescription for antidepressants and sent me on my way. This time, I started taking them straight away. To my relief, they took away the surface layer of pain, but they also numbed me to other emotions. But at that moment in time, it was a welcome respite. For the first time in a long time, I experienced a beige shade of hope.

As the fog of anxiety lifted, I recognized I was unfulfilled and unhappy with my job as a personal trainer at the gym. I decided I would start my own business. I was a specialist in pregnancy and postpartum exercise, and I had an urge to create something of my own and work within that niche. That was the beginning of my first self-employed venture, Fitbump.

As I began drawing up plans for my business, I started dreaming of a future. It was wonderful to feel like something more was possible. With that elevation of hope, I came out of my shell and started connecting with people again. I existed again. I laughed. I smiled. I was able to take Luke places without the intense feeling of dread that would come over me when I left the house. I still had moments sometimes in the middle of the night or late afternoon when the familiar tendrils of anxiety and depression would remind me they were still there. I would push them away. I would tell myself I was fixed. I was better now. I was on medication.

In April 2013, while I was at work, I had come downstairs from the gym to get a cup of tea from the café. As I walked back out toward the corridor, I was caught by a smile from one of the regular gym members, Tom. Sitting next to him was a man who I'd seen before in the gym, but never up close. *He's cute,* I thought. I didn't know what his name was.

Tom gestured. "Samala, this is Andrew." I smiled, and he smiled back at the very moment the butterflies in my stomach made their appearance.

Andrew was thirty-five, recently divorced, and had two sons. I was instantly attracted to him. He came across as open and chatty, asking lots of questions and showing interest in me immediately, which was something I wasn't used to. I had always been the one to pursue a relationship, often initiating and making myself available for the other. This time was different, and I was enjoying being courted. I noticed that he started coming in regularly when I was on shift and would seek me out for conversation while I was on the gym floor. I started wondering if he would ask me out for a date, and I soon began hoping he would. Then about a month after we had been engaging in regular conversation, the noticeable shift happened.

WALES, LATE APRIL 2013—AGE TWENTY-FIVE
I walk toward the gym exit; I stop as the double doors swing open. Andrew walks through, and immediately my heart beats wildly in my chest. And there it is, I sense the magnetic tension surrounding us as our bodies move toward each other almost like I am being pulled toward him. He walks right up to me, and we look at each other for a moment before we both smile. I notice his pale green eyes, the dark lashes that encase them, and the light brown soft curls tucked around his ears. His features are fine, almost elf like. *He is beautiful.*

"Alright?" he says.

"Yes," I say, a little too breathlessly as I stare at him eagerly.

"Where are you going?" he asks, and I detect a slight look of disappointment on his face.

"Oh, downstairs to the café to do a bit of admin," I answer, smiling.

"Okay, sounds good. Maybe I'll see you later," he says.

We both walk away, only to turn and look over our shoulders, our eyes meeting at the same time and exchanging a childish grin.

My heart skips a beat as I skip all the way down to the café.

And I'm gone, again.

WALES, MAY 6, 2013—AGE TWENTY-FIVE

I look out the window and see a blue BMW. I quickly check myself in the mirror. I have chosen a silk T-shirt dress with black sleeves and a floral pattern on the front, paired with black ballet pumps. I leave my flat and walk out toward the car. I see he is out of the car and standing by the open passenger door. He's dressed in dark blue jeans, a blue and white checked long-sleeve shirt and Nike high-top boots. *He looks very sexy.*

We drive to a cute rural town just outside of Cardiff. He parks the car, and we walk down the high street to the restaurant. Despite the evening sunshine, a cold wind blows up the street.

I shiver a little, and he puts his jacket and his arm around me. After we arrive at the restaurant and are seated, we talk nonstop about our children, the ending of our relationships, our families, and our past.

I don't pick up on the things he says, or rather the things he doesn't say. He talks about how his boys are his priority and how he values his independence. How he likes a "strong" woman. That he wants life to be simple. He tells me he has been seeing someone, but he has broken it off. She had wanted more—children, marriage, and commitment. I sense a tiny niggling feeling in my body, but I dismiss it. *She obviously wasn't right,* I think. We chat continually as the waiters bring us our food, and the night all too quickly ends. As he pulls up at my flat, I say, "Do you want to come in for a cup of tea?"

At 6 a.m., my alarm goes off. I look over at the man in my bed and smile.

I soon began to experience all the signs that I was falling for someone. I couldn't eat, my bowels turned to water, and my heart raced constantly. Something I discovered later in my healing journey was that feeling sick, not being able to eat, sleep, or drink are signs that your body is in fear. I just happened to equate them as love. My nervous system did not know how to attach securely.

After that first date, we went all in very quickly. "I love you" was exchanged within a few weeks, and we saw each other as much as we could. We introduced our children to each other the day after our first date. I was swimming in love hormones. Every now and then, my intuition fired a warning shot, such as when I told him I was taking antidepressants and he responded with, "But you're not down. Are you? You're a positive person. Aren't you?"

Sensing his discomfort, I began keeping my moments of anxiety to myself. I did my best to be "a happy person."

Whenever I told him I had a problem, he would always tell me to "look on the bright side." Eventually, I stopped taking my antidepressants because I felt ashamed for needing them, and I didn't want him to think badly of me. I did my best to have a positive outlook, but it became toxic to me. That kind of outlook had me suppressing any emotion but happiness.

WALES, AUGUST 2013—AGE TWENTY-SIX

SAMALA'S JOURNAL—AUGUST 6, 2013
"He asked me to move in with him. I am so happy. I love him so much. So much. Thank you thank you thank you."

TWO WEEKS LATER.
I pull the plug out of the sink and look over at Andrew as he says, "Do you think we should keep your flat?"

I knew this was coming.

"What do you mean?" I say as my stomach drops and my face starts to feel prickly.

"I don't know if living together *is* a good idea," he continues.

"What? But I've paid to end the lease on my flat, I…" I pause, tears start to prick my eyes. "Why don't you want me to move in? Have I done something wrong?" I ask as my throat becomes thick and tears fall.

"I like my own space, and I'm just not ready. But we will live together one day when the time is right."

I don't respond, I have no idea what to say and into the wall of silence he says, "I really like it when you come to visit me."

Anger and confusion blur my vision. I take my half-drunk cup of tea and walk out of the kitchen and into the backyard.

My mind turns over what he just said, and something sticks out like a shard. *Visit him… What does he mean by visit him*, I wonder. That's not intimate or representative of the closeness we have shared over the past three months. I hold my cup of tea in between my hands and look up at the trees as thoughts fly around in my mind. *I feel so humiliated. I knew it was too good to be true. He's discarded me, just like that. And now I have nowhere to live.*

As soon as he said his piece, the conversation was over. On reflection, I have often thought I should have left then and there, but I didn't and allowed myself to be held at a distance for nearly three years. I believed I was crazy and something must have been wrong with *me*. That if only I could be *better*, he would commit to me. After that conversation, everything changed. Sometimes, when I was driving to his house,

I would experience unease at the thought of being there and feeling unloved or simply tolerated, but I couldn't not go. I was completely addicted to the emotional pain that this relationship fed me.

If I expressed any low mood, anxiety, or sadness, he would say, "Don't be such a downer." The signs were all there from the beginning, but it just took time for me to see them. I accepted that he never stayed the night at my place, and I would do my best not to show my desperation to see him. He would tell me I was being "needy" if I asked for reassurance, and paradoxically the more he told me I was being needy and withheld himself from me, the more needy I became.

The moments of love he seeded to me were precious, and I would lap them up, hold on to them, and like prayer beads I would turn them over and recite every loving thing he had done to try and soothe my aching heart.

SAMALA'S JOURNAL—DECEMBER 2013
"I must resolve to be more busy, ordered, and positive. My procrastination causes my despair. I feel like I am never a part of my life, that I exist on the outskirts. I'm not really here."

WALES, AUGUST 2020—AGE THIRTY-THREE
I opened my eyes and looked around Sian's treatment room. My eyes were drawn to the window, where I could see the sky, which was a soft pale blue. I watched in a semi daze as birds dove from tree to tree. The rolling hills behind the houses opposite made a serene backdrop. I sat up slightly

and dropped the soft blue blanket that was covering my body down a bit. I reached over to the side table and took the cup of water Sian had left. I drank eagerly. My body was light and tingly. My head pounded slightly as I thought about what I had seen and experienced. I had cried out. I touched my face to see if it was still wet with tears. My lips were salty where the tears had flowed down during the reiki session. The door opened, and Sian came quietly back into the room and sat down on a low stool in front of me.

"How are you feeling lovely?" She smiled as she spoke.

My voice cracked a little as I said, "I don't know. I cried a lot, I think. I felt a lot of heat and tugging around my womb. So much sadness there."

She nods. "Mmmm, I was really drawn to your sacral chakra and womb space. Your womb was heavy and holding a lot of dense energy. I saw the image of babies and mothers. I felt a lot of resistance to letting go and opening."

"That's interesting. I had a painful experience with a past partner, and I wonder if I am still holding on to it. It was a while ago, but I think it still bothers me. I still feel guilt and sadness when I think about it and perhaps some anger."

"We have time now if you would like to talk about it," she spoke.

I moved forward and began to tell her about Andrew.

WALES, MAY 2015—AGE TWENTY-SEVEN

I stand in the kitchen of the tiny flat that my son Luke and I live in. I hold my iPhone in one hand, the other resting on my belly. My thumb is poised over the call button. I close my eyes and tap.

My heart moves rapidly in my chest, and I nearly lose my nerve and end the call, but he answers before I do.

"Gorge?" *Andrew says*, using the nickname, short for gorgeous, that he'd chosen for me.

"Hey," I say, my voice choking slightly as I speak.

I am silent for a moment as I lean against the bench and look over at Luke. He is sitting on the sofa, eating pasta and watching *Transformers,* his little face so focused on what is happening. *Ideally, I would have liked this conversation to be private, in person, and on a day when Luke is at his dad's, but I can't wait any longer.*

I return to the moment and clear my throat.

"I'm pregnant," I say and hold my breath.

No sound comes from the other end, but I immediately sense the volume of his feelings. It rises and the full force comes out through the phone at me.

"Are you fucking *kidding me!*" he screams. "Are you fucking kidding me! How did this happen? I thought you were on the pill! You're having an abortion! We are not keeping this baby! I *don't want it!*"

Great heavy sobs break through as I try to still myself in the wave of his reaction. I quickly walk out of the kitchen and into my son's room as it's further away from Luke.

"I can't have an abortion. Please, I can't. I won't. I don't want to," I whisper firmly into the phone.

Tears are falling, but a resistance pushes me into action. I plead with him, "I did not plan to be pregnant, and the pill isn't 100 percent. I love you, and I love this baby. Just like I love our children. Please, Andrew, I don't want to."

"Then we are finished." And he ends the call.

I stare down at my phone in disbelief. The whole room sways as a tide of panic threatens to engulf me. I'm reminded of a time earlier in my life, grasping at my mother not to leave me and to let me in the car. A voice in my head pleads, *Don't leave me. I'll be good, just don't leave me.*

Frantic energy pulses through me as I call him. The first few times he doesn't answer, so I keep calling until he does.

"There is nothing to discuss," he yells at me.

I cut over his angry voice and speak.

"Please come here so we can talk about this. Please, I'm begging you." Tiny sobs escape my mouth as I do my best to be quiet.

Luke is still in the living room, and I don't want him to hear my distress. My mind rips itself apart trying to work out how to fix this. *I don't want to hurt Andrew. But I do not want to have an abortion. I want the baby but don't want to lose Andrew.*

Eventually, I hear a quiet knock at the door.

I open the door. He stands there for a moment, white faced. I've never seen him so angry, and as I look down, I notice his hands are clenched into fists. Again, the thoughts tumble. *I don't understand why he is so angry at me. I know it's not what he wants, but to end our relationship if I don't have an abortion seems like an unbelievable reaction.*

Andrew walks into my flat, and Luke looks up. He's pleased to see him and runs over. Andrew picks him up, gives him a hug, and sets him down.

"Time for bed," I say and walk Luke to his room, which is but footsteps away from the living room in the tiny flat. "Couldn't swing a cat in it," was what the owner had said. I look back at Andrew, but he's not looking at me.

I shut the bedroom door and read Luke a bedtime story, trying not to cry as I feel the tension in my body building. I'm scrambling in my mind for things to say while I attempt to read at the same time. Luke finally falls asleep. I get up off his bed and tiptoe out of the room.

Andrew is standing in the kitchen with his arms crossed. I look at the expression of fury burning on his face and my intuition says softly, *Maybe now is not the time for this conversation.* But I persist and put on my best grownup voice because at this moment I feel like a child who has done something bad, and I am about to be punished.

"I don't want to have an abortion, but I also don't want to hurt you, and I don't want to lose you. I love you."

I move toward him, softening myself, but he steps back.

Between gritted teeth he says, "I don't want another child."

Sensing a threat, my hand instinctively goes to my stomach.

"Don't do that," he snaps at me.

I drop my hand.

"Please," I whisper. "Please don't make me do it."

"I'm not going to make you do it, but I'm not going to stay with you if you don't. I'll do the right thing and pay child support; I'll do my bit, but I want nothing to do with you or the baby."

I look up into his face.

"Are you seriously telling me that you will have nothing to do with your own child?"

"I don't want it. I don't want another child. You said you didn't want any more children. You said that to me. You lied to me!" he says hysterically.

"Now that I am pregnant, I realize that I *do want another child*, with you," I plead, and I do. I really do. I want his child. I thought I would be okay with not having any more children, but everything changed the minute I saw the double lines. I thought of Luke with a little brother or sister. I saw us living together. I saw us getting married. I saw us being a team. I saw the united and loving family I wanted with him.

"Don't you remember when we went out for dinner not all that long ago and you told me maybe you would like to have a baby with me? Don't you remember sitting there, holding hands over the table, and talking about our future?"

"Yes, and I also remember the following morning saying that I took it all back!" he spits.

I can feel I am losing a battle. I don't know what else to say, so I stand silently.

Until he fills the silence for us. "You're an idiot. You're ruining your own life. You're making the wrong choice. You'll be a single mum to two children. I don't want anything to do with you, and I don't want anything to do with the baby."

He turns away from me and walks out of my flat.

CHAPTER 9

Blood

—

In my blood
I found,
her

WALES, JUNE 2020—AGE THIRTY-TWO
I waited for the quiz results to show on my laptop screen.

DISORGANISED/ FEARFUL AVOIDANT ATTACHMENT STYLE

An attachment style that develops when a child's parents or caregivers, the only source of safety, become a source of fear.

Something clicked inside me. Followed by a deep exhale.

WESTERN AUSTRALIA, AUSTRALIA, 1992—AGE FIVE
I wake suddenly with alarm and look around. My baby sister, Una, lies sleeping next to me. We are alone in my parents' bed. *Where is Mum?* I wonder. Immediately, my face starts

tingling, followed by a sick feeling in my tummy. I climb off the bed and run down the hallway into the living room. I see the orange glow of the heater and think she must be in there. But the room is empty. The babysitters are gone, but they left the heater on. I start to cry. I run into my room to see if she's sleeping in there. She's not. I run into Una's room to see if she's sleeping in there. She's not. I run back out into the living room in case I didn't see her asleep on the couch. She's not there. I run into the kitchen, the bathroom, the laundry. She's not there.

I open the front door and look out into the darkness of the front yard. I run to the back door, but it's locked. I run back and kneel by the heater in the living room, pushing both of my hands in between my knees and curl forward saying, "Please Mummy, where are you?"

I don't know how to call Dad and wish he wasn't away, I think as I look around the living room. "I'm scared," I say out loud and continue to rock back and forth.

Then hear my sister cry. I run back down the hallway and get under the covers with her. I hug her and hold her close. I get back out of the bed and run back to the living room, kneeling and pleading for my mum again. I run, back and forth to the living room and my parents' room until the sun starts to rise, and I fall asleep next to my sister from sheer exhaustion.

WALES, MAY 2015—AGE TWENTY-SEVEN

He isn't coming back. I rock back and forth on the floor in child's pose. Quiet sobs continue to escape me. "Let me back in," my heart pleads. "Don't shut me out."

I had thought Andrew would come back. And as time went on and he didn't come knocking, the full force of what had happened hit me. Our relationship was over, and I was pregnant with his child. My inner strength and conviction over keeping the baby was waning, and the blind panic I was experiencing was dialed up. I understand now that I wasn't having an anxiety attack as such, but my body was interpreting him leaving me as a severe threat to my survival. Even though I wasn't in physical danger, I was losing the person my nervous system had equated with safety. The more he pulled away, the more I wanted him, and I would do anything to stay with him.

Once again, I had become a version of what someone else wanted and not who I *was*. I wasn't honest with him about what was important to me, what I wanted, and how I was feeling about our relationship. But I didn't know how to be. So, as I lay there, paralyzed in fear, all that mattered was unbreaking my heart and finding a way to fix what I believed I had broken.

The door to him was locked, and I was scrambling around in the dust for the keys.

WALES, 2015—AGE TWENTY-SEVEN

I pace around the flat like a frantic animal. I throw up multiple times and wring my hands, and I am assaulted by a severe headache. My chest tightens, and I don't know what to do with my body, so I eventually sit on the floor and hug my knees. *Why does everyone always leave me?* I ask of no one.

I call him, over and over, but he doesn't answer. I no longer feel like an adult but instead a small child, and I will do anything to feel safe again. I get up off the floor, bundle my sleeping son into the car, and drive to his house under the cover of darkness. It takes me fifteen minutes to get there. I park my car on the street near his house and gently pull Luke, who is still sleeping, into my arms. I knock quietly but repeatedly on his door until he opens it. The anger on his face is palpable, and as he looks at me, I imagine myself through his eyes—pathetic, weak, and completely desperate.

I begin to cry as I say, "Please let me in. Please can we talk?"

He opens the door wider and lets me in.

I walk upstairs and place Luke, still sleeping, in the bed that he slept in when we stayed over. I head downstairs, breathing in tears, and take a moment to compose myself. I find him in the living room and see that he is perched on the end of the couch. I turn to jelly, I can't stand seeing him so angry, and I fall to my knees by his feet.

"Okay, okay, okay," I sob. "I'll do it, I'll have the abortion." I am desperate for him to pick me up and hold me. *Why won't he hold me.*

"I just want us to be together. I want you to be happy," I whisper.

"Get off the floor," he says.

As I stand, I move my body near his but sense his resistance. I search his face, but I see a distance in his eyes.

"Can I have a hug?" I ask in a small voice.

He places his arms around me and draws me in, but an invisible wall stands between us. So fractured we are unable to connect. So, I take my pain and bury it deep. At least he is still here. And I praise myself for being a good girl.

SIX WEEKS LATER

I close my eyes and place my hands softly over my belly as the familiar feeling of nausea washes over me. I try not to think about tomorrow. Instead, I speak out loud, in a whisper, to the little embryo in my belly. "I am so sorry. I hope you can forgive me. I love you; I hope you know that. Please come back when the time is right."

Why can't this be taken out of my hands. Please take it out of my hands. I don't want to go through with this, but I'm not brave enough to say no. I'm not brave enough to do it on my own.

I fall asleep hoping for an answer to my prayers, but I wake up with the reality of my choice weighing me down like the deepest ocean. Andrew and I get into his car and drive into the city center.

I feel like I am going to my own execution. We walk toward a building nestled in among the high street shops. You would never know the abortion clinic was here. People rush past us, and the man walking next to me chats away as if this were any other day and we were out for a pleasant stroll. Little shards of hate gather in my heart as I look at him.

We enter the building and take an elevator a few floors. The doors open, and we walk out into a corridor. Up ahead of us is a woman sitting behind a desk. I look around. There are no pictures of smiling babies here, only empty dull walls. It's like a space of limbo: blue plastic chairs, glazed windows, and closed doors.

Why is this not more comfortable? It's like they are trying to make this as awful an experience as possible. Even if this was my wholehearted choice, it is the hardest choice that any woman will have to make. She could at least have a comfortable chair to sit on. I'm in my own thoughts when I realize he's paying the bill. He enters his pin, looks up at me, and smiles as if he is buying me a gift. I look at him through narrowed eyes as we go and sit down.

"Samala."

I look up to see a woman standing in a doorway. *She must have come from behind one of those closed doors.*

I stand up and walk over to her, and she guides me into a small room. She closes the door behind me, and I stand for a moment, not knowing where to sit.

"Take a seat, sweetheart," she says and gestures toward one of the blue plastic chairs. Two chairs separated by a small table with a box of tissues on top. I notice more boxes of tissues stacked underneath the table.

I sit down and automatically place my hands over my belly. I am aware that I am round already. My body has responded quickly to the pregnancy hormones.

"Okay, Samala, I'm Leanne. I'm the clinic counselor, and I am here to ensure this is something that you do want to proceed with. I'm going to ask you a few questions, and then I'll open the space for you to talk me through how you're feeling. Then we'll go from there. Okay?"

I smile and nod.

She proceeds to ask me questions around my safety. Am I being pressured? Is this my choice? And I hold my nerve as I hold back tears and say it is my choice all the while thinking, *But I have to because there is no way I can make her understand how important the man out there in the waiting room is, and I am not strong enough to have this baby against his wishes. I don't want to, but I don't have any other choice. I am so angry, but I also love him in equal measure, and I can't believe this is happening.*

I leave the tissues untouched and walk back out of the room to sit down next to Andrew.

He looks over at me and says, "All good?"

"Yep," I reply shortly.

Then he takes my hand is his and says, "I was thinking you look very nice today."

It takes all my strength not to walk out of the clinic.

A nurse in white and blue walks out from another closed door and calls my name. Andrew squeezes my hand and releases it. My stomach flips as I push down the urge to say I can't do it.

I walk across the room, my stomach lurching as the room spins. I feel as though I am no longer in charge of my body. The nurse closes the door and gestures me toward another plastic blue chair. I have another conversation where I barely know where the responses come from, but then I hear her say, "I'll need to do an ultrasound to see how far along you are."

A flashback of my first ultrasound with Luke jumps into my mind, and an intense pang of longing threatens to swell up out of me. *I am going to see my baby.* I walk over to the bed and lie down. She places the cold gel on my stomach and runs the ultrasound transducer over my stomach. She pushes into my abdomen and turns the little monitor away from me.

"Can I see, please?" I ask.

"Are you sure?" she asks kindly.

"I am, please."

She turns the screen around. My breath catches in my throat, and a sob escapes as I stare at the little shape hovering around on the screen. Tears stream down my face and a crushing weight presses on my chest. *Stop, stop, stop,* a voice whispers. *I can't. I can't. I can't,* says an even louder one.

"You're just over seven and a half weeks," she says as she turns the transducer off and wipes my belly.

"Okay," I say, gulping. The tears won't stop, and I start to shake.

She looks concerned as she says, "Do you need to take a moment? Do you need to talk to someone?" She hands me a tissue and places her hand on mine.

I shake my head and blow my noise. I can't find the right words. "No, it's okay," I say, sitting up and pulling my jeans on.

I walk back over to the plastic chair, and she sits down opposite me. She takes a file, and I watch as she staples the ultrasound pictures in. But unlike the last time, when I was going to keep my baby, she turns them over and pins them face down.

"Can I have one?" I ask.

"Of course," she says, opening up my file and cutting one out.

I look at it for a moment and then fold it up and place it in my bag.

"Okay," she says. "I'm going to give you two pills and then you're going to go home. As you are under ten weeks you can have the loss at home. You may find things start happening within two hours, so you need to get home as soon as possible."

I look down at my feet as she speaks. I don't feel real. None of this can be real. But then she hands me a paper cup with water followed by a little cup with two pills in it. I hold the little cup in my hand and then look at her.

"Let me give you a moment," she says, standing up and stepping out of the room.

I continue to stare at the pills, grappling with my mind, and then I take the little cup to my lips followed by the cup of water.

I let out an audible cry as I hold my stomach and whole body tight while I lean forward and let out a quiet howl. Then I catch my tears with a tissue, wipe my face, and disconnect from my body.

I hear a knock at the door, and then a second later the nurse walks in. I notice she is holding a white paper bag.

"All done?" she asks.

"Yes."

As I stand up, she hands me the paper bag. I look inside to find a leaflet detailing what to expect, a pad, and pain killers. *A goody bag. This is all so wrong.*

I walk out into the waiting room and Andrew stands up with an unreadable look on his face. I see he is holding a vasectomy leaflet in his hand.

A little too late.

I don't say a word as we walk back through the city center. I wrap my arms around my body and coil inward. Dread surfaces as I begin to feel the familiar sensation of my uterus twinging. I avoid looking at him as tears start to fall. I know he doesn't like it when I cry. We reach his car and get in; I wipe my face and feel him looking at me.

"What do you want for dinner, gorge?"

"Um, I don't know, maybe roast chicken and potatoes?" I say, but all my attention is on my belly and the waves of shame, anger, and sadness rolling through my body.

"Okay, I'll go past the shops quickly," he says and starts the car.

My eyes are shut, I have been somewhere else in my mind. I open my eyes as I feel the car stop, and then hear, "I'll be quick."

Andrew gets out of the car. It's raining, and I watch him pull his jacket over his head as he runs into the shop.

Little pangs flare like tiny fireworks deep in my belly. The last thing I want is to be in the car when it starts. I look out the window at the little droplets that cling to the window. Through the foggy window, I see him jogging back to the car with a shopping bag.

"Let's go," he says, and we drive back to his place.

His cheery disposition slices through my heart. *Why is he so happy?* I wonder.

He pulls up outside his house, and I get out of the car quickly. I stand behind him as he unlocks the door and then push past gently and run upstairs. I take my clothes off, get into one of his old T-shirts and climb into "my" side of his bed. I hear his footsteps as he comes up the stairs, my eyes follow him as he walks over to sit by me, on top of the blanket. Something about this makes me think of a child sick in bed with a cold. He hands me a cup of water as I take the painkillers out of the paper bag.

"I'm going to go and make dinner. Call me if you need anything," he says.

"Please stay with me," I say as I hold on to his hand, but I can sense him pulling away.

All I want is for him to lie down next to me and hold me.

"Call me if you need anything," he says as he leans forward to kiss me on the forehead.

I curl onto my side and wait for the inevitable. I want to cry but nothing comes. I am frozen in time until I feel the first pang. It reminds me of the first time I experienced contractions. Luke's face surfaces in my mind. *You are disgusting,* and I turn my mind to the man downstairs and pray, *Let everything be fixed after this.*

I sit up as the pain intensifies. This is really happening, and I get out of the bed and walk to the ensuite to sit on the toilet. My body is hot in sharp contrast to the cold toilet seat. I grip the sides, white knuckled, as great crashing waves move through my body while it lets go of its creation, blood running, my heart breaking as I seal my truth away.

I love him. I. Hate. Him.

I stand for a moment, staring into the blood. I want to reach in, I want to take that blood and smear it all over my body. I want to take it back into me. I don't want to let it go.

"I'm so sorry," I whisper. "Please forgive me." I pull the chain.

I walk downstairs showered, clean, and feeling nothing.

"I think it's over, the main part," I say, standing in the entrance to the kitchen.

He walks over and hugs me. I put my arms around him. I don't cry. *I will be brave; I will be brave for the both of us. I want him to see how brave I am.*

"Dinner's ready," he says, releasing me and bouncing back into the kitchen.

Silently, I sit down on the couch, and his dogs jump up on either side of me. He comes back into the room, passing me my food and asking, "Shall we watch a film?"

And we didn't speak of it again until months later when the full force of my grief, rage, and loss came bubbling up and protected me when I needed it most.

CHAPTER 10

Dead Heading

Until you pull the monster
Roots and all, out
Of the wound that it grows
You'll continue to battle
The same monster
In many different forms
It's not enough to dead head
And drop your sword victoriously
Because another will step forward
and take its place

SAMALA'S JOURNAL—AUGUST 2015
"Today my heart aches. I don't know how to be. How do I be with Andrew? I don't know if he really loves me. I don't know if he really chooses me. I don't think he wants to. I am always on the outside. I think it's making me mad, and I keep dreaming about being pregnant. I wake up and I am holding my belly."

WALES, JULY 2015—AGE TWENTY-SEVEN

In the weeks and months after the abortion, Andrew and I returned to a state of detached equilibrium. We stopped talking about the future. I made no plans with him in my mind. I expected nothing from him, and I went into a dream like state. I shifted from anxious attachment to my own version of avoidance. I simply started closing myself off.

The intensity of my pain and my feelings of abandonment and rejection needled into my heart and grew like a sickness that spread throughout my body. I would often find myself feeling so incredibly angry at him. I withdrew my love, I withdrew my affection, and I am sure, on some level, he sensed it. It was as if we were caught in a sort of inertia. Neither of us knew how to talk about what we were experiencing, but we stayed in the familiar momentum of our relationship.

Then one day, as I was browsing at my local bookshop, a book *Eat, Pray, Love* written by Elizabeth Gilbert caught my eye. I had been to the cinema to see the film when I was pregnant with Luke many years before. Knowing how much the film had touched me then, I knew I had to read the book now. As I dove into the book, something began to open within me—a feeling that I had experienced before. When I had believed I was trapped and had no choice, I remembered I did have a choice and I was strong, very strong. I did not have to stay in this relationship. I did not have to be in any relationship.

WALES, JUNE 2020—AGE THIRTY-TWO

The clock on the dashboard flashed 1:20 p.m. I leaned back into the driver's seat of my car, closed my eyes, and continued to speak to Liz.

"I did the attachment style quiz yesterday. My result was anxious avoidant, which makes a lot of sense. I can see why I did a lot of the things I did and attracted the people I did. I wonder, especially when I think about my time with Andrew, if he had an avoidant attachment style. I mean I can't know that for sure."

"It's possible, and possibly you amplified the opposites within each other. You may well have had the same attachment style. Has this helped? Learning this about yourself?" Liz asked gently as her voice floated through the speakers in my car.

"It just set some things in place for me. I understand why I spent half the time fearing a lack of intimacy and connecting but fearing letting go into intimacy and connection. But now I get it. I suppose it's just where I go from here."

WALES, NOVEMBER 2015—AGE TWENTY-EIGHT

Andrew and I sit together eating dinner on his couch. I look over at him and breathe deeply, I have been building myself up to this moment. I needed to tell the truth. I needed to know what is happening with our relationship and, crucially, does it have a future I want? *You already know the answer. You just want him to confirm it.*

"Andrew, do you think we will live together soon?" I ask, as I place my knife and fork down.

I watch as his body tightens at my question. He stays silent, and the pause is excruciating, but I wait. Finally, he answers, "No, I know you want to, but I'm just not ready. It's not the right time." He looks away.

I want him to make eye contact with me. I can't read him. *Where is the open, loving man I met almost three years ago? Did I make him up?* I wonder.

"Not ready," I say in a whisper. I harden myself, exhale, wondering why I'm doing this.

"Andrew, we've been together for almost three years, so please tell me when you think you will be ready." I look straight at him as I speak.

"I'm just not ready, you know, with my boys and doing my own thing. Surely you understand?" he says in a defensive tone.

Don't fight it, says the intuitive voice. I inhale and look into his eyes, trying to work out what he is really feeling and really thinking. Is he scared? Is it me?

"Okay, fine, if that's what you want," I say, and I am surprised at my lack of tears.

No more holding on. I sense the final tether holding me to him snap.

"I'm sorry, gorge. I'm just not ready," he says, almost pleading.

I can tell he is uncomfortable since I know he doesn't like conflict. He places his hand on my leg and squeezes. He leans forward to kiss me.

"It's okay. I understand," I say. "It's fine." Both of our attention returns to the TV.

I disconnect myself from my love to him. I don't know how I do it, but I always find the ability to turn it off, eventually.

A few weeks later, I was due to go with him to his parents' house for Christmas. But at the last minute, I decided I wanted to go and stay with my sister, Hayley, in London. She was traveling and currently living and working in London. Andrew showed no outward signs of caring when I spoke with him about it. I didn't have Luke that year for Christmas, and I didn't want to go with Andrew and pretend everything was okay. After that conversation about still not living together took place, the festering anger and resentment shot to the surface.

I was prepared to be alone on Christmas Eve for the first time in my life rather than go and be with him and his family. A simmering anger and glaring resentment about the abortion was always a few centimeters below the surface. And as the months had gone by after the abortion, I would find myself thinking about the baby that could have been, especially as the month, January, that he or she would have been born neared. So, as I withdrew, so did he. A thick glass wall stood between us, and I had no idea how to break it, nor did I know if I wanted to.

On Boxing Day, the day after Christmas, *we came together with the kids and exchanged presents. I knew the moment he opened the front door to let me in that our relationship was over and had been over for a long time.*

Andrew and I sit quietly on the living room floor as the boys, his two and mine, play on the side with the PS3.

We both hold our cups of tea and sit in an awkward silence. Andrew is first to speak into the thickness.

"I'm upset that you didn't come with me for Christmas. My mum had made Christmas pudding especially for you."

I shift my body slightly on the floor to face him.

"I know. I'm sorry about that. I didn't give much warning. But I think we need to talk," I say in a low voice, mindful that the boys are not far from us. I summon the courage to take the next step.

"I'm not happy, Andrew, and I don't think you can give me what I need," I say. It feels odd to be saying this after so much time together.

"I know," he says and shuffles toward me slightly. "I'm just not ready for commitment. I'm not ready to live with someone, and I don't want to get married."

I notice he doesn't say anything about children.

Laughter threatens to erupt—sometimes I do that in awkward emotional situations—but instead I say, "I know."

I can't be bothered fighting anymore. All the fight has gone out of me.

That night, we had sex. I knew we shouldn't have. It was like a final goodbye. It was so sad as I opened to the sadness in his body and experienced sadness for him. I knew something was deeply wrong, and it had nothing to do with me. With that a resolve formed, I decided it was no longer my task to make him love me or to heal his wounds for him.

The next morning, I stood on the doorstep of his front door while Luke and his boys ran around the front garden. The winter sun shone down on us as we said goodbye. It was such a strangely unemotional parting after almost three years together. I turned to wave at them, and then Luke and I got into my car and drove off.

WALES, JANUARY 2016—AGE TWENTY-EIGHT

I hear the message alert on my mobile go off. It's Andrew. *I haven't heard from him since Boxing Day and now he's messaging me?*

Andrew: Can I come over? I'm just around the corner.

Me: Sure.

Why would he be just around the corner? It's nowhere near his work or home.

I quickly run to the bathroom and check myself in the mirror. *Why do you even care?*

Two minutes later, I hear a knock at my door. I tussle my hair and take a deep breath. I open the front door and examine him. He's lost weight. His face is drawn. He looks sad, but I don't feel sorry for him.

I open the door wider and say, "Come in."

I turn and walk toward the kitchen, and over my shoulder say, "Tea?"

"Sure," he says, closing the door behind him and following me.

I stand by the kettle and place teabags into mugs. The air is heavy, but I don't say anything. I'm waiting for him to speak.

Eventually, he breaks the silence and says, "Is there any way we can fix this?"

"What?" I say, not looking up. But of course, I know what he's talking about. Irritability ripples through my body. *We broke up. It's over. End of story.*

"Look, I've been doing a lot of thinking, and I want to be with you. I want to see if we can fix this," he says as he moves his hands to indicate the both of us.

I turn to face him straight on. "No," I say as I hand him the cup. I place my cup back down on the bench because I am concerned I might throw it as I can sense the anger flaring.

He needs the whole truth.

"I can't forgive you," I say looking into his eyes with a steady voice.

"For what?" he asks as he clasps his cup of tea.

"The abortion," I say with as little emotion behind my voice as possible. As angry as I was, I was still rattled by the thought of our baby, and I did not want to cry in front of him.

"What do you mean?" he asks with a confused look on his face.

Seriously?

"You told me if I didn't have an abortion, you would leave me. I didn't want the abortion. You knew that, but I did it because I didn't want to lose you. I wanted that baby, and *that* baby would have been due in a few weeks' time. And you certainly didn't support me when I had the abortion. You pretended like nothing was happening. We never spoke of it. Even when I had to go back because I was still bleeding weeks after it happened and had to have D&C! You acted like it wasn't important."

He makes a face that looked like a child's when they were caught drawing on the walls.

"You left me all alone, Andrew. You never even asked me how I was—not after, not ever." I continue, "You acted as if it never happened." I let out an exasperated sigh and walk over to my couch. He stays standing where he is.

"I'm sorry. I just wanted to get you through it. I didn't want to dwell on it. I was shocked about you being pregnant too," he says avoiding my gaze and moving to sit on a chair across from me.

"That's not enough. I felt I had no choice. It wasn't truly *my choice*. We never had an open, compassionate conversation about what we both wanted. You left me when I needed you the most," I say.

"I didn't mean it. I wouldn't have really left you. I was just angry. I was in a panic. I would have come around. I thought you would have known that," he says, almost childlike.

It takes me a moment to register what he said. *Did he really just say that?*

"*Oh my god, Andrew!* Did you actually just say that! Do you know how that makes me feel? That's even worse. Please. Just go." I stand up. My entire body shakes as the months of grief and pain swell within me.

What would our baby have looked like? Sickness and rage fill me.

"Please, go," I say as I stand and push at him with all my energy.

He stands and moves back toward the front door. I walk forward, pushing him out of my space.

"Okay, I'll go. But please, I want to be with you. I want us to be like it was at the beginning when we would eat chocolate off each other's bodies, when you would leave me notes telling me how much you loved me. I want to take you on holiday and make you smile. Just think about it, please," he says, almost pleading. Then he opens the door and walks out.

Eating chocolate off his body is the last thing I want to do. I lock the door after him.

The amount of strength it took for me not to call him in the moments after still amazes me. All I had ever wanted was for him to want me. There he was, wanting me. But I had this inner strength, this resolve. I didn't know where it came from, but I clung to it with all my might. The rage that filled me was a protective rage. He was not coming back in. But as the universe would have it, I would face one more final test. Was I finally ready to step into a higher level of worth?

A FEW DAYS LATER
I hear a knock on my door. *It's him.*

I open the door just by a crack and peered out at him. *Why is he here so late? And why is he wearing a suit?*

A little whisper echoes in my body. *He's going to propose.* I *then* notice that one of his hands is in his pocket.

"What do you want, Andrew?" I say, drawing my shawl around my body, shivering.

"I want to try everything, and I haven't tried this, so I want to ask you something," he says as he moves his body as if to come in. He is also smiling, so sure that I am going to let him in. I stand my ground and keep the door slightly ajar. He starts to take something out of his pocket.

My eyes narrow. "Don't. You. Dare," I say. "Don't you *dare* propose, when you know it's all I ever wanted, when you had so many moments. Don't you dare do it now."

"Please, gorge, let me," he says, his face looking slightly pained.

"No, Andrew. No. Go away." *I shut the door on him.* I stand, shaking with my hand on the door handle. My heart pounds in my chest. I listen to his footsteps as he walks down the pathway. I wait to hear his car door open and the engine start. When I hear him drive off, I exhale deeply and slide down the door to sit on the floor. Adrenaline is coursing through my body.

Did that just happen? Did I do the right thing? Yes, a quiet voice answers. *Yes.*

CHAPTER 11

Permission to Feast

―

I've put on the red shoes, many times
Danced until I bled
And cut myself off to heal
But I didn't learn
And along came another carriage
I dissolved again
Turning to red shoes,
Again again again
Spinning, bleeding, braking
One last time
I begged for the axe
To sever it once and for all
I sit weaving now
My own handmade shoes

I have always had a raw hunger within me, but good girls are not gluttonous. They do not feast, and they do not make anyone feel badly. They wait for permission. They carry guilt like a suit of armor, and most importantly, they must always make their mother happy.

WALES, JUNE 2020—AGE THIRTY-TWO
"You've been through a lot, Samala. Complex trauma is like having thousands of tiny cuts all over your body that have never completely healed. It's going to take time. Are you being kind to yourself?"

I took a moment to reply to Liz's question. I'm sitting in my car with the windows down. The UK was experiencing a record-breaking heatwave. I didn't mind it, though. I turned my face to absorb the warm rays.

Truthfully, I replied, "I'm trying."

WALES, JANUARY 2016—AGE TWENTY-EIGHT
Once again, I escaped a relationship and ran, eyes fixed forward. I did my best to forget about the past three years. I never saw Andrew again after that night. Within weeks of disentangling myself from him, I intertwined myself with Jacob, who would go on to become the father of my daughters. We met through work, and while my relationship with Andrew spiraled to its end, a burgeoning friendship with Jacob grew. My gaping wounds were patched over with new love, and I threw myself into the next chapter of my life.

I told no one the truth about what had happened with Andrew. I had told some that I had experienced a miscarriage, and the shame of that lie spread like poison ivy through me. I had nowhere to grieve my lost baby, and I just wanted to move forward as quickly as possible. I kept so much of what happened to me jammed down within, and with no idea of how to start being honest, I burned everything down and started again. Vulnerability was a word that did not exist in my vocabulary. My relationship with my mother, even my father, was filled with half-truths. And it was very much how it had been since I had left for the UK. We did not really connect. I played a part.

It was so easy for me to disconnect from my family, especially my mother. A part of me knew I had wanted to put distance between us, and another part of me dismissed it. I was busy. I had Luke, my business, and now, a new relationship with Jacob. I fell into the ease and flow of Jacob, and we moved in together within six months of our relationship starting. He was steady, and when we well fell pregnant with a girl, Isla, toward the end of 2016, and there was no questioning that she would be born. But the undertow was there waiting to rise and take me down with it.

When Isla arrived earthside in August 2017, we were joyous with love for her. But the undertow rose within weeks of giving birth to her when I finished breastfeeding and returned to taking antidepressants. They rendered me torpid, and I moved through life in a daze as the antidepressants turned my colorful emotions to gray. But I was functioning, which mattered most to me. We made plans to buy a house and planned to have another baby. But there I was, once again, trying to be someone, trying to build a life when I had no idea who I was. On the outside, I presented as someone who had it all together, but on the inside, I was a complete wreck. Even the antidepressants couldn't numb all the pain.

The tugging feeling remained. The further I played the role of mummy, partner, businesswoman, good daughter, and good girl, the more severe my emptiness became, and the more extreme the coping mechanisms. I went from the occasional binge to weekly binges followed by purges. I exercised constantly and obsessed over how healthy my food was. I bit my fingers and fretted in the middle of the night over everything and nothing. I was completely disconnected from myself. If someone was to ask me what I wanted, or what was wrong, I couldn't have told them. I did not know who I was, and I had entombed *her* deep within me. As the ghost within me raged with hunger, I returned to the doctor and asked for my antidepressants to be increased until I reached the maximum dose and became a senseless, empty vessel.

WALES, JANUARY 2019, AGE THIRTY-ONE

I sit on the floor and wrap my arms around my knees. I bury my head in my legs and cry. As I rock back and forth, I'm aware of noises coming from downstairs.

"Where's Mummy?" I hear Isla ask.

I hear footsteps coming up the stairs. I reach out to place my hand against the door so she can't come in.

"Mummy, where are you?" she asks.

I sniff back tears and wipe my face. My lips feel puffy. "I'm just on the toilet sweetheart, I won't be long."

"Okay," she says, and I hear her walk away.

I stand up and wash my face in the sink. I clean the toilet, wipe the seat, and am sure to get rid of any evidence.

"This is the last time," I say out loud. "You can't keep doing this."

I get up off the floor to look at myself in the mirror. I look sad. I look puffy. *I want to be someone else. I don't want to be me anymore.*

You secretly need me, an insidious voice in my head says. *You don't really want to get rid of me.*

"It feels good to get it all out. It feels good to feel alive."

A hunger that had existed since childhood consumed me as it blazed into adulthood—a hunger for more. I was metaphorically starving, but I feared the hunger that ripped through me, the hunger that morphed into binging and purging. The combination of numbing myself so completely to bringing myself fully awake after the purge. It was addictive, the cycle of feeling so low followed by the high of adrenaline after the purge.

For a long time, I did not recognize that I had an issue. When I spoke to my therapist about my behavior, it was not as black and white as bulimia, but rather the purging had come about years after my disordered relationship with food and my body had begun. It was escalating because my mind needed more and more ways to escape and numb. The pain within me was spreading and the dopamine chase was elevating.

So much of my perceived salvation was rooted in how my body looked and how small it was. If I could get my body "just right," all my stresses would be gone, and I would be "happy." I was infatuated with the idea of being perfect. But ironically, I had no idea of what that form was.

If I caught my reflection in the mirror, my mind would focus in on all the parts I loathed, and despair would strangle me. In that moment, I would resolve to eat less, train harder, and stop being so weak. And even when I was at my "fittest" or "best shape," I did not stop to appreciate it because I feared it would be taken away from me. So I chased the next look, the next gym program, the next healthy eating plan. Working in the health and fitness industry only compounded this drive because I had an identity to uphold, a look to maintain. But it ran deeper than that. I was deeply unfulfilled and was filled with ideas about success, life, and happiness that did not belong to or originate from me.

Food had been a fixation from childhood. I recall drawing up mental plans about how I could break into the local supermarket and steal all the Mars bars. I became so enthralled by food. What did other people eat and how much? What kind of treats did they get to have? What kind of food did they have in their house?

All my emotions and how I coped was entangled with food and eating. When I was sad, I ate. When I was stressed, I ate. When I was happy, I ate. When I was angry, I ate. And then, later in childhood, I learned I might not get another meal like the one I was having. I might not get to eat, and being hungry became a fear. This only continued to reinforce the belief that I would never get what I wanted, whether it was food, safety, or love. It simply was not for *me*.

I did not realize I had been blaming myself for my mother's and everyone else's actions my entire life. If I had been good, if I had been better, if I had been more loveable and enough, then they wouldn't have done the things they did. If I could only fix myself, get rid of all my broken parts, I would be happy and life would be perfect. This unseen perspective had been playing out in my mind for the better part of thirty-two years. This narrative was the root of many of my thoughts and beliefs that I held not only about myself but the entire world. Because everything I believed within, I was projecting without.

WALES, DECEMBER 2018—AGE THIRTY-ONE

Since moving from Australia to Wales, I had been back to visit my family on average every two years. As we—Jacob, Luke, Isla, and I—prepared to travel back in December 2018, tension was building within, and perhaps it had been there every time, increasing as the years went by. Months before we were due to travel there, I had the thought, *This is going to be Mum's last Christmas*, in the back of my mind. She had been diagnosed with muscular dystrophy when I was around thirteen. The news had been another thing that created a well of worry within and anxiety. In truth, I pushed down that knowledge and ignored it as best I could for most of my life. I knew eventually she would need support, looking after, and retrospectively, did I leave Australia to run away from the pressure of it? Perhaps. The type she has is a very rare and slow-moving type. But in 2018, things had ramped up with health complications presenting.

As the year unfolded, conversations turned toward this being her "last Christmas." I felt a deep discomfort within. I had accepted her illness, but the inconsistency of the information unsettled me. I never fully knew or trusted that everything I was being told was true. But I went along with everything being said. I struggled with guilt whenever I thought about my sisters. I knew when things became challenging, when my mother needed more help and support, the three of them would be picking up the pieces.

The pressure to have a wonderful time, a perfect Christmas, to play happy families and for us all to be together was there as soon as I arrived. But I also felt the underlying darkness always shimmering and hovering in the background. And maybe it was mainly me, but I walked on a tightrope of tension that could break at any moment, an eruption of tears, yelling fueled by misplaced envy or jealousy from my mother aimed at us, normally me and my sister Una. We were very close, especially as we both had children. Our bond had grown in adulthood, and not that I was not close to my younger two sisters, but when I had moved to Perth when I was nineteen, Una had followed not long after.

As if she sensed the building tension in me, after having a couple of glasses of wine one evening, my mum made light of my experience of being left by the roadside. Not without venom, she said in front of my whole family as we were all talking in Una's living room, "Oh we all know why Samala is *so* anxious. It's because I left her all by herself when she was three." She took a sip from her glass.

To this, no one really said anything, and I quickly changed the subject. I always had the niggling feeling that I really was broken. Why couldn't I just pull myself together and get on with things? But that comment fed the fire that was burning. Deep within me, the anger that I did my best to repress began flaring.

WESTERN AUSTRALIA, DECEMBER 2018, CHRISTMAS EVE—AGE THIRTY-ONE

I sit cross-legged on the floor in Una's room, surrounded by presents that still need wrapping. I hear the door open and turn to see Mum as she walks in. A wave of irritability ripples through me as I glance up at her.

I do not need words, or to have laid eyes on her to know the look that is on her face—pursed lips, a downcast smile, and an energy of deep sadness and frustration that wafts in as she does. My body stiffens in the presence of that energy, and I know what she is going to say before she even says it.

"Why didn't you make me a picture like the one you made for your dad?"

You sound like a child, I muse as my stomach turns over. I don't want to fight.

I think of how stressed Una is at making this the perfect Christmas for her because we all have the weight of the "last one" hanging over our heads. Una has been running around buying all these presents for her, out of fear that Mum will be disappointed if she does not get all she wants on Christmas morning.

I turn my body to her. "Mum, that's the only present we could think of to get for dad. And we have so many other presents for you. Una has been doing so much to make sure you have everything that you want."

She sits on the edge of the bed, facing away from me and says, "But I would have liked that too."

I exhale, deflated. *Nothing we ever do satisfies you. You never feel loved enough, never important enough.*

"Mum, we all love you, but nothing we do is ever enough," I say, and deep within, a little voice questions that. *Do I really believe that? Do I love her?*

She doesn't reply but continues to sit on the bed.

I continue to wrap presents, and I look around, feeling exhausted by the sheer number left and wondering why she is still in the room bothering me. *I just want to be alone.*

The heavy silence bears down on us, and eventually she takes her disappointment and sadness out of the room. I sit there, letting go of the scissors, and fall into the whirlpool of thoughts. Why is nothing we ever do good enough? It always ends up like this, us looking after her, loving her, making sure *she* is okay. *This is why I moved to the UK. I ran away from this.* The familiar sensation of anxiety builds in my body, my chest tightening with a lingering pressure in the back of my head. *What can I do? How I can I make this better?*

My mind races, attempting to piece all the puzzles together. I try to separate all the broken bits and fit them together so they make something neat in my mind, but all I keep coming back to are the unsaid, unexpressed emotions. The cloudy memories, the pretending, the play acting at being a "happy family."

But underneath, everything is so deeply wrong, and I don't want anything to do with it. I pick at the side of my thumb, distracted, and then a packet of chocolate snowmen that are meant to go in the children's stockings catches my eye. Adrenaline surges. Two minutes later I stuff the empty packet into my pocket, walk into bathroom, and lock the door.

CHAPTER 12

Righteous Rage

―

I accepted my pain.
I said come in.
What do you need.
And I became my own divine mother.

WALES, APRIL 2020—AGE THIRTY-TWO
I hit send on the message to Una.

Me: I think I'm having a psychological awakening.

She replies quickly.

Una: That sounds fun. I want one.

Me: You don't. It's awful.

Coming to realize the reality of what had happened to me as well as the feelings toward my mother and myself were some of the hardest parts of the journey. I had an untapped reservoir of anger swelling within me. And anger is one emotion, especially among women that is not "acceptable," and it certainly does not align with being a good girl. Thirty years of repressed anger was a bomb waiting to go off.

Throughout my whole life, I had known something was not "right," but I always came at it from a perspective that it was my job to protect her and, in a way, protect myself.

As I unraveled my past, uncomfortable feelings of guilt and regret started to surface. I swayed between anger and regret, occasionally finding myself wishing I had never opened Pandora's box.

SAMALA'S JOURNAL—APRIL 2020

"It's like my mind is trying to tell me it didn't happen. I feel guilty for even thinking about my mum as a bad person. I feel sorry for her. I think of her all alone, and it breaks something inside of me. At the same time, I am so angry. I am so trapped in this loop. I was feeling so good and now I feel like I am going back to square one. I don't know how to love me."

I was struggling to love and accept the little girl who believed she was unlovable. And the pain of having no mother was far worse than having a mother who couldn't love her in the way she deserved.

In 2019, when I was ten weeks pregnant with my third child, I traveled back to Australia with my daughter Isla, who was around eighteen months at the time. In those two weeks, the enormity of my anger, resentment, and deep-seated trauma surged forward like a tidal wave. I had stopped taking my antidepressants. Paradoxically, I had hyperemesis gravidarum and was throwing up multiple times a day. I was constantly triggered by the interactions with my mother on that trip. I did not have the energy to pretend or to buffer my mother's actions anymore. Perhaps it was because I was no longer numb, and the thinning of the veil between my subconscious and conscious mind that allowed my true feelings to push through.

Throughout the entirety of this pregnancy, the internal tugs increased, pulling me toward a remembrance. I can see that it had to begin with the realization of what had happened to me. It was a very intricate shedding process that required time.

I heard the quiet whispers within saying, "Look here. Look within your heart. Look deep beyond your mind and into your body."

AUSTRALIA, WESTERN AUSTRALIA, MAY 2019—AGE THIRTY-ONE

I sit in the passenger's seat of my sister Una's car as we drive to visit our mum. Isla and Finley, Una's son, are in the back singing nursery rhymes.

My hand rests on my belly as the car journey causes the nausea to increase. I marvel at how I'm only ten weeks pregnant yet feel as sick as I do. *It is worse this time.*

As we drive, I reflect on the weekend just gone.

I, along with Isla, my sisters Una and Hayley, and my mum had just been away for the weekend. It was one of the most awkward, tension-filled weekends I had ever experienced. We had stayed in a cabin about two hours south of Perth. From the moment we arrived, I felt a divide, mainly between my mum and me that I had not noticed before. I didn't know if it was the pregnancy, but I was less patient and found myself biting back at behavior that I would have previously ignored.

The sharpest being the way she commented on Isla's behavior, "Oh she's just like you were when you were a child," whenever she displayed less than desirable behavior. She was also incredibly unempathetic about my hyperemesis with remarks like, "I was never *this* sick when I was pregnant," as if I was making it up. And, "If you feel this sick now and can't cope with Isla, how are you going to cope when you have a baby?" To anyone else, it may have seemed inconsequential, but I heard the barbed tone to it, an undercurrent of cruelty that set my hackles to rise.

So, as we near Mum's house, I begin to seethe. *I don't want to see her,* I contemplate.

I shield my eyes with my hand as the morning sun shines brightly. As the car pulls up on the drive, I continue to muse, *I don't have the energy to pretend and be nice today.*

I get out of the car and walk around to get Isla and Finley out of their seats.

The two cousins toddle up to the front door as Una and I walk behind.

Mum opens the door. "Finley!" she exclaims, picking him up and making an overt fuss over him.

What is going on? I wonder as she essentially ignores Isla.

"Hey, Mum," I say as I walk up behind Isla.

She looks at me with a tight expression. I can sense it already—the bitterness, the disappointment, the "why don't you love me" energy.

I want to leave; I don't want to be here. I feel strange, not like my normal collected self. An image of a lioness backed up against the wall flashes in my mind, and then a whisper from within signals something is coming. Anger is building, and I don't know if I can control it. I remind myself, *Anger is the one emotion you can go to jail for, it's perfectly fine to be bitter, to be grumpy, to be frustrated, but anger is never okay, anger is not allowed.* I remember being little and hearing her say, "Don't you get angry with me," whenever she had done something to upset me or if I was taking a stand for myself.

Una and I walk into the living room and both fall onto the couch to wait as Mum goes to get changed. We're going to breakfast, but she's still in her pajamas, even though she knew what time we were coming. Little things like that are sticking out to me. Una and I talk quietly. I am swimming in the emotional storm that rages around us. I know Una can feel it too, but she remains in a calmer disposition. I, on the other hand, am preparing for the battle I sense coming.

Mum walks around the corner. And on her face is *that look*. Pursed lips, eyes pinched, and a disappointment that emanates from her.

"Why don't you love me?" she almost whines as she stands before us.

My heart starts beating wildly. I practically jump off the couch. *This time she is going to get the truth from me.*

"Are you serious, Mum? Are you actually serious?" I say in a high-pitched tone. My throat burns and tears threaten.

"Yes, you were awful to me all weekend," she replies defiantly, almost like a child.

"Oh my god, Mum," I say, sounding like my teenage self. And then, something breaks inside of me.

"You know what? You know what? I don't love you. I can't stand you. I *hate* you. You have no care or thought for anyone else. You didn't even buy Una a birthday card. You didn't say thank you for the weekend. You brought *no* money. You never have any money. Why is that, Mum? Why are you so incapable of looking after yourself and us?" My voice elevates as I speak, I lose all connection to who and what is around me. I am cloaked in red.

Her eyes glaze over as her face goes white and then red. She starts to walk away from me, leaving the living room where Una is now on the floor with the kids, but I follow her.

"No. I won't listen to this; I won't listen to what you have to say," she replies indignantly with her back to me.

"Yes, Mum, you *will* listen because none of this is right. None of this okay. How you act, how you treat us, it's not normal! You lied about being sick, the whole "last Christmas" palaver. I came back here, at ten weeks pregnant, on a seventeen-hour flight, with a toddler because *you* told me you were dying. That it was imminent, but you're not dying. You always want more. More love. More attention. It's never ever enough and I want to know *why!*" I scream.

I ignore how my body starts to ache as I walk after her. I follow her down the hallway toward her bedroom. I just want her to listen to me, to say sorry, to apologize. I don't really know what for, but something feels deeply wrong, like I am scratching at the surface of a festering wound. I can feel the emotions, but I can't see anything. I am just so angry, and I want *her* to make it better.

"Get. Out. Get. Out of my house," she shrieks at me.

She walks into her bedroom, and I follow her. She turns to face me and spits, "*You* are a bitch. You are a *bitch*! Now get out of my house!" she screams.

"I hate you," I yell. My arms are around my body, holding myself together. Tears prick my eyes, and I can't stop them as they stream down my face. I always cry when I get angry, and it makes me angrier as I feel as though it's a sign of weakness.

I realize Una is hovering behind me, and I remember Isla. *Where is Isla?* But then my anger takes over.

Mum looks at Una, twisting her face from hate to pleading. "Please, Una, take her away from me. Take her away."

"We should go Samala," Una says quietly and edges out of the bedroom.

I am locked into my mother with so much anger within me. I don't want to leave, but I don't want to stay.

She stands in the corner of her room, her face sharp and pointy, her dark eyes glaring at me. Her lips are thin as she practically snarls at me, "Get out, you bitch."

"I will never, ever, ever speak to you again," I say coldly and with as much force as I can.

I turn to walk out of the bedroom and find Una at the front door with the babies. We all get into the car, and as I sit down, I feel that my knickers are wet. My chest starts heaving and the tears come with full force. Panic and fear erupt. I take my hand to my belly. So much emotion.

I call Dad to tell him what happened because I know she will be on the phone to him just as fast, and he will get a twisted version. I don't understand what just happened, but for the first time, a crack appears within my mind. Something is wrong. Something is very wrong.

Thirty minutes later, we all arrive at a café. I leave Una with the children and run to the toilet. Hardly breathing, I close the cubicle door. I am terrified that all the anger, resentment, and emotional upheaval of that confrontation has caused my little baby to want to leave me, but there is no blood. I realize that I had wet myself, and relief rushes through my body as I sit down on the toilet. I place my hand on my belly. "I'm so sorry little baby. I'm so sorry," I say.

In the days after that confrontation, my whole family dynamic blew up. I could see that Una and my two younger sisters were stuck in the crossfire. While I was able to leave the country and get away from her, Una was there in the same city and with a life that included my mother. A divide appeared, and it became very clear to me that speaking out about my mother and the experiences I had had with her, speaking my own truth, was going to have an enormous rippling effect.

Emails went back and forth, and when I reread them, I could see how full of anger I was. The turmoil and anger in me demanded something far greater than a simple apology. I know now that nothing my mother could ever say or do would lead to my healing, but I had to discover and accept the parts of myself that I had rejected out of internalizing messages about my sense of worth due to her actions. At that point, I was not clear on what had really happened. All I knew was I was angry.

I was still looking out and seeing the external experiences, situations, and people that were causing my "unhappiness." I was yet to connect the dots and see that my anxiety, my chronic stress levels, my disordered relationship with food and my body were all symptoms of an underlying root cause. My repeated traumatic experiences were yet to be processed, healed, and released. I had a web of negative core beliefs running deep within my mind, and they were running the show.

Even the way I had confronted my mother had come from a fight response. We were never going to arrive at any resolution that way, and quite possibly, at the time, I did not want to. Letting go of my anger toward her has been an integral part of my healing journey. But I did have to feel all of it first. I had to allow the little girl, the teenage girl, and the adult in me to be angry because she was. I was angry at not having a loving and caring mother. I was angry at not having my needs met. I was angry at not having the support I needed as I went through high school. I was angry that my parents had separated and went about it so terribly. I was angry at all the mistakes I had made. I was angry at the people who had hurt me and rejected me. And I was very, very, angry at myself.

By mid-May 2019, I had left Perth to return to the UK without speaking to my mother, and I remained fixed in my decision not to speak to her again. At that point, I did not believe I had any work to do. I did not realize I was severely traumatized, and I believed the solution to all my distress was her saying sorry.

But the inner turmoil that presented at not speaking to her weighed heavy, and true to my disorganized attachment style, I could not stay distant from her for too long. I also hated being the cause of a "divide" within my family. I didn't want to displease anyone. I knew how uncomfortable everyone was.

Within a few months, I reached out to her, apologized for my behavior and getting angry, and we resumed the status quo. I took all the blame and felt ashamed for my erratic outburst. I pushed everything that had risen back down inside and ignored it. But something had indeed changed. Something had shifted within me. Despite it not coming about in the best way, that expression of anger and speaking in part, some of my muddled truth was the first time I had done so. A crack formed, an opening, for life to begin working through me.

And the rage that filled me had burned through the first layer, and what had been revealed to me on that trip could not be unseen.

CHAPTER 13

The Cracked Vessel

In her eyes
I saw my death
Cracked open
My body
The wreckage
Weaved back together
Anew

Birth is a profound and transformational experience. Pregnancy and birth are sacred rites of passage that a woman may move through in her life. Every pregnancy is different as is every birth. And at each birth, not only the baby but a mother is born. When birthing, a woman straddles the liminal space between life and death. Her body the vessel, the sacred portal where new life emerges into the physical world. Each of my births were different, shaping me and changing me in unseen ways. Each of them opened, strengthened, and delivered me into my own womb space, where I emerged a new version of self, stripped of all that I was, stepping out raw and fresh, just like the new baby suckling at my breast.

HEATH HOSPITAL, WALES, NOVEMBER 24, 2019—AGE THIRTY-TWO

"Samala, be careful. You'll sit on her," a voice pierces through the invisible veil that is separating me from my body, where I am floating in the darkness, and pulls me back to the present moment.

She's here, I think and become instantly alert and stop myself from rocking too far back on my heels. I look down to see the tiny baby coated in vernix and blood. I reach in between my legs, placing my hands around her tiny seal-like body. She makes no sound as my hands connect with her, and I move her out from underneath me. *She is perfect.* She stares up at me, and I gaze into her eyes thinking they are like pools of black water. Then I see that one eye is bloodshot. Underneath her, I see the blood covering my knees, and watch as blood continues to soak and spread, like an opening flower, on the white hospital pillow. *I am so thirsty.*

I gently draw her up to me and feel the tug of the umbilical cord deep within my belly. I look over to her dad Jacob as he comes to cut the cord. I watch as if they are on a movie screen while the midwife, who had been there for the birth, hands him something that does not look like scissors to me. After a moment of him fumbling and slipping, trying to cut the cord, she hands him the correct tool. She apologizes, and Jacob separates my baby from me. I bring her further up on to my chest. I inhale her and think she smells like earth after a summer rainfall. But then my attention shifts to the room around me, which is beginning to spin and fray at the edges.

I look over at the midwife and ask, "Can I get up on to the bed now?"

"Of course," she says and begins to ready the bed for me.

I manage to climb up onto the bed, keeping the baby in my arms, and lie back on a pillow. I position her on my chest, and she burrows, finding my nipple easily. She drinks deeply, and I sigh as the relief of the connection washes over me.

I am so thirsty and why is no one bringing me water, I wonder.

As the baby feeds, I look around. People are moving quickly in and out of the room, more people than before. *Something is wrong.* I glance over my right shoulder at Jacob and see that his face is pale. Then I look over to my left and see "800 ml blood" written on the white board.

"Can I have water?" I say, as my voice cracks but no one responds.

Then a lady—a doctor, I presume—appears by my side. After a moment, I realize she is speaking to me.

"We need to examine you; you are bleeding more than we would like, and we need to find out where the blood is coming from. Is that okay?"

I nod, but I don't really understand what is happening.

I wince as hands go inside my raw vagina, pulling and pocking at swollen and stretched flesh.

"*Ow!*" I yelp as a hand goes in my bottom. I begin to cry, and I look down at the top of my baby's head. *So much hair.* Then someone pushes down on my stomach, and I close my eyes and focus on breathing. *Still no water, I am so thirsty.*

The same lady as before appears by my side and speaks, "Samala we are concerned that your uterus is not contracting as we can't find any other source of where the blood could be coming from."

A coldness enters my body as I look at her face. She looks worried.

The midwife unlatches the baby from my breast and takes her from my arms as the doctor continues to speak, "We need to put you on a drip with Syntocinon, but if that does not work, we may need to take you to theatre."

I nod at her but am distracted by the midwife who is now swaddling my baby and placing her in the little incubator crib. My body starts to shake uncontrollably, and I notice a sour taste in my mouth. *This is bad. I'm going to die.* I say goodbye to Isla and Luke as someone puts a catheter in my hand, and I stare at the sleeping bundle in the incubator.

Then the room begins to close in on me, and my heart yearns to hold my baby as I slip into oblivion.

Seven months earlier, after the confrontation with my mother, the tiny cracks started appearing. They came in the form of questions. They came in the form of memories. Where I had previously been able to force myself to push through anxiety and low moods, I was no longer able too. Where I had previously been able to silence the parts of myself I did not like, they refused to keep their mouths closed. Everything I had been stuffing down made its way to the front of my mind and demanded to be seen. Like a spinning top, I was losing momentum, and I could no longer keep up the act. The funny thing was, I did not even know I was acting. I just knew I couldn't go on.

The pregnancy with Meredith awoke long sleeping parts of me. Her soul was a powerful, fiery presence in my body. Our mutual fires came together to burn through everything that no longer served me. I do not believe it is a coincidence that my moon is in Sagittarius, and she a Sagittarius sun, and that her moon is in Leo and I a Leo sun. The moon sign in astrology represents the body and emotions, and I know she was sent to assist in awakening me to the power of my body and my emotions.

After the trip to Australia in 2019, I knew something was deeply amiss, but at the stage I did not have the strength to create space between my mother and me or even step away for a period of time to look within myself. And after we resumed our "relationship," it had a different tone to it, but I was unaware of what it meant to be enmeshed, or of what it meant to be attached so much to someone and want to get away from them in equal measure. She was my tragic love story.

From as young as I can remember she would ask me, "Do you love me?" I would always answer, "Of course I love you. You are my mum." I could have never given an alternative answer because I had never contemplated there could be one. All I had wanted was to feel love and acceptance from her, and I learned to believe that love included a mixture of fear and safety. Ironically, it did not make any difference, no matter how much I loved her, told her I loved her, did things for her, made myself small, allowed the violation of my boundaries, I would end up feeling hurt by her, only to be asked, "Do you love me?" The belief that I was never enough was engrained so deeply I knew no other way of being.

As I moved through the pregnancy with Meredith, I oscillated between a numb haze and intense anxiety attacks. My body dysmorphia and eating habits plummeted and were only exacerbated by the hyperemesis gravidarum. Most days, I would wake up and tell myself I needed to pull myself together. *You have everything you want, so what's wrong with you?* I would think. But it was as though I was holding all the pieces of a tattered tapestry and doing my best to weave them together. For what and for whom, I did not actually know. Everyone remarked on how "together" I seemed, congratulating me on my beautiful family, my new house, and my business, but the inside of me was far from cohesive, and all I wanted to do was hide.

So, I distracted myself by being "busy" with my children, with work, with exercise and my endless pursuit to look a certain way, and with looking after my house. I struggled to maintain close friendships because I was never sure if anyone wanted me around. If I had a moment when I expressed a low mood, or a seeming "negative" emotion, I would experience a backlash of more fear and anxiety. I didn't want anyone to know I was sad, stressed, and not "okay." I did not know at the time that I was already at rock bottom and still a little way to go before I would eventually resurface. I did not know that all the "mental health" problems I was experiencing were symptoms.

Compounding all of this was that I was still in a rigid relationship with the person who had been, and in many ways, was a main source of fear. Although she was far away, I was stuck on a trauma loop and even the sound of her voice created a visceral reaction within my body. And any display of anger, manipulation, or control, although it was more subtle and likely completely unconscious from her part, would send me into a tailspin. But at that point, I was so adept at disconnecting from my body and used to the background hum of anxiety, I didn't notice it.

It took the traumatic birth of Meredith to fully break me open. Within an hour of giving birth to her, I came very close to dying. As my body leaked its lifeforce, I lay on the hospital bed, whispering my goodbyes to my children while Meredith slept in her father's arms. I was reborn that night, and I left the hospital a completely different person, not me, and not yet the awakened me. I was in a cocoon of birth trauma. Hovering above my body, triggered relentlessly until I could take it no more and wished I had died that night. As I sank down into the depths of the postpartum haze, I was yet to unravel and face the truth of the relationship with my mother, my past, and most of all, myself.

WALES, APRIL 26, 2020—AGE THIRTY-TWO

"Well, my mum, she did things, and I feel, I don't know. Like some of things that she did and happened weren't loving."

"Okay, tell me. What things did she do?" Liz asked gently.

I started crying. My throat was tight. I was on the edge of remembering something important. I told Liz about being left by the side of the road. That was always *the* memory, the one that stood out the most.

Then I continued, "But…" and I paused as I whispered, "I also remember being hit… pinched… I remember being strangled and suffocated. I remember crying and saying no. I remember her hurting my sister Una. And it never stopped… there was violence but that wasn't all. As I got older it changed… there was drinking and… just this feeling of always worrying. I could never relax. I became responsible for her and my three younger sisters, even more so after my parents separated. And even now, I have just this weird feeling, like I want to speak to her, but then sometimes I wish she didn't exist. I have memory gaps. Other things happened, not with my mum, but I feel like I am so broken, and no matter what I do, I mess everything up."

I put my hand over my mouth. I shouldn't be saying these things about her. They were in the past.

"Tell me how you were responsible for her?" she asked, a soft nudge in her tone.

"Well, Mum has depression. Sometimes she wouldn't wake up in time to get us to school, so I started getting up and making sure we were ready. Sometimes we would have no money, so I would remind her to buy food. Sometimes she would drink and get angry, so I would hide the keys so she couldn't drive off. Her behavior was, is, unpredictable. I'd listen to her as she would tell me her worries and concerns. I'd remind her to pay the bills, things like that."

"And how old were you?" she asked gently.

"I suppose this started quite early on; I mean at times I was left alone when I was little. But the responsibility, eleven perhaps, but it was in full swing by the time I was twelve."

"And where was your dad?"

"After my parents separated, he worked away, for two weeks at a time, and then he came home for a week or so. But he didn't really know what was going on, or maybe he did. I'm not sure. I don't know why. No one really knew what was happening. I never had friends over. I never spoke about it. I always wanted to go to other people's houses."

"Samala, do you think this experience, what you have experienced is normal?"

"What do you mean?" I asked. My heart was thumping in my chest. Guilt was piling up in the back of my mind.

"Well, do you think the environment with your mother was a safe and functional environment?"

"I suppose no, but it wasn't her fault. She was depressed, and she had had a tough childhood, and I know I was difficult as a child." I was feeling defensive. This wasn't what I wanted. I just wanted to stop binging and purging.

"So, you blame yourself for your mum's actions?"

"I guess. I mean, if I had been better, perhaps things would have been different," I said.

I had this gnawing feeling in my stomach. *Do I really believe that?*

"Samala, I think we have a lot more to explore here. I am going to send you a trauma stabilization pack. From what you are describing, you have experienced multiple adverse childhood experiences and have been repeatedly traumatized. This is what we call complex trauma. Compounded with your other life experiences, it is understandable that you are suffering so intensely right now," she said.

"Okay, if you think that will help," I said. I was happy to be led. I just wanted someone to tell me what to do so I would feel better. *Isn't trauma for people who had suffered things like war?*

We wrapped up our session, and as always, she said, "Take care of yourself," at the end.

I didn't know why, but that made me feel uncomfortable. *Why would anyone care if I took care of myself,* I wondered. I got out of the car and the whole street moved sideways. I went into my house and ran straight up to the bathroom to vomit. This time it was not me forcing it. My body was cold and shook violently.

I went and curled up on my bed. I closed my eyes and repeated, "I'm safe. I'm safe. I'm safe," as tears rolled down my cheeks. The cracks, wide and deep parted my entire being.

CHAPTER 14

Untethering

―

Mother, this time I cannot stay
I cannot be the daughter, you wished me to be
As my heart opens to heal
it tells me it is time
to let you go
and finally choose
me

My nanna loves to remind me, whenever it is my birthday, of the year I turned three.

Reminiscent, she speaks of me running around with glee and telling anyone who would listen "I'm free. I'm free."

In the year I turned thirty-three, I discovered the freedom that had silently been within me all this time

"I'm Free."

WALES, LATE MARCH 2020—AGE THIRTY-TWO

After that call with Liz, I curled up on my bed and waited for the sickness to subside. In that stillness, a sensation of hope began to expand within me. A glimmer, a tiny spark shimmered in my heart. Something more was at play here. Desires and aspects of myself that had been suppressed or that I had been afraid of showing started to step forward out of the shadows. My connection to self, spirituality, intuition, and other darker parts of myself dared to move into the light. This time, I saw them. God, the universe, source, whatever you want to call it, had always been a prominent thread throughout my life. Many times, I had leaned into spirituality in different ways.

But in 2020, my first "dipping my toe in" spiritual act was buying a set of goddess oracle cards. I remember when they came, the excitement that rippled through me as I read through the book and gazed at each goddess. What followed was my first reading, and an initiation into that part of myself that had lain dormant for so long. Other modalities such as astrology, human design, and energy work called to me—all tools for further understanding the self.

But then came *the work*, and alongside working with Liz, I consumed everything I could find about the psyche. I followed the thread deeper into my inner world. I wanted to understand myself, and I wanted to pull back as many layers as possible. I felt an insatiable hunger that presented, and I wanted to go into the dark, dank cellar. I had already hit the lowest ebb; how much lower could I go? I wanted to untether myself from all the places, people, and ideas that were choking the life out of me. I wanted to pull out all the bodies, all the parts of myself I had exiled to die over the past thirty years.

When I first started working with Liz, I didn't tell anyone apart from my father and my partner Jacob. I was hesitant because I was waiting for someone to tell me I wasn't allowed to do the work. That I wasn't allowed to access my own past, confront it, and dissolve the trauma that was still living in my body. Roughly a year after the confrontation with my mother in Australia, I began this work. I started feeling uncomfortable about talking to her because I was digging up so much. I found when I spoke to her, I would pretend to be okay.

I couldn't talk to her about any of it. Often when I did broach something, she would shut it down or minimize my pain, telling me my memory wasn't correct or that it wasn't as bad as I was making it out to be. I know it was difficult for her, but at that point, I was fragile. I wasn't in full strength, and our conversations would only trigger me into a more severe binge and purge episode.

Revisiting my past created a wedge of conflict within me because I couldn't understand how you could say you love someone, as my mother always had, and then treat them in the opposite way. My thinking was still very black and white. I could not hold those two truths in balance. And a day came when I realized I was still putting someone else's feelings above my own. I was still putting her needs first.

I came to realize that I could not heal, express my anger, or be honest with myself if I was still pretending to be someone for her. And I did not feel safe to be angry, process, and be honest in her space. It was a challenge to speak my truth because not everyone had seen the version of her that I had. I had to let her go.

SAMALA'S JOURNAL—JUNE 2020
"It was incredibly painful sending that email to Mum, but I knew I needed to do it. I needed to figure out where she ended and I began."

An integral part of healing was allowing myself to grieve the childhood I never had. I had to pull off the Band-Aids and clean out the festering wounds that were deeply lodged within me. Only then could I start looking at the past with a different perspective. I also became aware of the web that ran from my mother into all my past relationships, choices, and actions. I was just facing the same monster, the same wounds, in different people.

Everything I was continually trying to escape shifted form. I thought about how I had allowed myself to be treated and had accepted behavior that was far from loving. I also saw how I treated myself. I never sought to love myself and accept myself. It wasn't about blame. I did not blame anyone, *but* I became aware of the way I had internalized past actions, which were now operating for the most part unseen within me. Only I could heal what was occurring inside of me, and that meant I had to stop running.

Early in our sessions, Liz recommended we work through a book together called *Mothers Who Can't Love* written by Susan Forward. It put words to the shame and guilt I experienced at confronting my own pain. Somehow by questioning my mother's behavior, I was going against society, against everyone. But it was vital for me to travel back to the moments that stuck out like shards of glass all over my body. I knew I wanted healing, but what I found was so much more precious—my own wisdom and my own self. Every single one of those painful experiences had two sides, and behind the pain, I was learning something about myself. And growth, as hard as it could be to accept, happened in those most pressurized of moments.

I had known of my mother's own emotional pain my whole life before I knew my own. Every time something happened when I was a child, even as a teenager and young adult, I had a difficult choice to make—to realize she was deeply struggling and not okay or believe I was doing something wrong. My brain had chosen that I was at fault long ago. From a child's perspective, it is far safer and necessary from a survival standpoint to believe something is wrong with you than the caregiver. And when I looked at my children, I did not want that same fate for them.

Working with Liz, followed by the other teachers and healers, allowed me to finally see my truth of where I had come from and why I was suffering so much internally. The space was finally available for me to start learning about who I was, what I needed to shift within me, and what I wanted for my life. As this work began, I dove deeper into discovering the source of the knowing, the voice that had pulled me back on that dark night and so many times before. I rediscovered my connection, my soul, my spirituality, and it was like magic. Things started "opening" up to me: people, places, books, messages... everything leading me to the next part of my journey.

Over the four months of working with Liz, my body eased. The cycle of binging and purging lessened, and I was able to interrupt most cycles when triggered. I began to feel love, for the first time in my life, for my body. I was clearing out all the mold and mildew that had been growing inside of me. With the pressure of having to leave the house, "show up" being taken away due to the lockdowns, I was able "fall apart" and explore the exiled pieces of me. While the pandemic was raging outside, I was experiencing the most profound and transformative experience inside. I saw I had no love for my business. I wanted to move on as something else was calling me. A new expression, a new way of being.

I enrolled in a women's health coaching certification and functional nutrition certification and came to understand the workings of the mind and body on a whole new level. Both professionally and personally, I was gaining a knowledge and experience in momentum that enabled me to see past the thoughts and beliefs that were casting a shadow on my life. I began letting go of relationships, situations, and ways of being. I began to remember my worth, which was hinged on nothing other than simply *existing*. But one day, after those months of working with Liz, I knew it was time for me to move on. Our time together had come to end, and it was beautifully timed. The next opportunity for growth presented itself.

All the while, I tended to the little girl within me. At times, I was afraid. Letting go of the relationship with my mother was difficult. I had to hold my little self through the moments of grief. I told her I had my own children, and I would look after her as I did my own. She was hesitant to let go and stop waiting for "Mummy," but eventually she came with me. And my inner child, my authentic inner child, is fun, joyous, adventurous, curious, and so loving. I feared these parts the most.

I had denied myself of my own comfort. I had denied myself the love and nurturing I had needed because I believed it could only come from someone else. As I brought more and more of my inner child online, I had a deeper level of compassion and understanding for my own children. I could sit with them in their pain without feeling triggered—still a work in progress, of course. Rather than dissociating whenever my two-year-old had a tantrum, I was able to be with her and hold her through her own emotional storms.

I was able to understand my mother's actions. I was able to see her pain and let go of the perception that her behavior was because of *me*. I was not at fault began to sink into my bones.

WALES, JULY 2020—AGE THIRTY-TWO

I wanted to intellectualize my healing, but some things couldn't be intellectualized. What I was yet to discover and wake up to was my body, but deeper than that, my energy body and the realization that my "mind" was not just up in my head but existed in every cell of my body.

Trauma does not solely exist in the mind. And emotional pain is stored within the body like a charge. That emotional pain is energy, which requires releasing. I was yet to connect my physical pain and my hormonal imbalances with the extreme chronic stress I had been under. I was still viewing the mind and body as separate entities, but soon I would unlock the truth that it is all one. I was soon to experience my body, and my energy, in a completely new way.

I knelt on the floor as I faced the computer screen. I smiled at the faces looking back at me. I'd been leading a beginner's virtual course in mindfulness and meditation. As everyone was still in some form of lockdown, my sessions and courses were being held over Zoom.

"Let's do a quick recap on the week. How is everyone doing? How did you do with creating the time and space to meditate and do the mindfulness exercises?" I asked. I sensed some hesitancy from the group so I continued.

"So, as you all know, this is new to me too, and I have to tell you all about this fascinating experience I had when I meditated this morning." Pausing, I closed my eyes and recalled the moment.

"During meditation this morning, I noticed a buzzing sensation throughout my body. At certain places, especially around my solar plexus and heart, I felt a rapid spot of intense activity. It was the strangest thing. So I googled it, of course, and what I learned was that energy can get trapped in certain spots around your body. I had no idea, so I am curious to find out more. Has anyone else had this experience?" I asked enthusiastically because I really was intrigued by what I felt, and I had a sense of knowing that I needed to follow this thread.

One of the women in the group put up her virtual hand and took herself off mute.

"I had a similar experience, and I found out it was trapped emotional energy that had not been released from my body," she said.

My surprised and interested face was reflected to me on the screen as she continued, "I ended up going and having reiki with this amazing woman. Her name is Sian, and she's a reiki master with a whole host of skills. It transformed my life; I would highly recommend getting in touch with her."

"Reiki," I said. I had heard of reiki and knew it had something to do with chakras, but I was yet to discover just how pivotal this would be to my transformation and healing.

After the session, she sent the details for the reiki healer. I called her immediately as I knew intuitively it was the next step. Sian's voice over the phone was warm and safe, and as I shared some of my story, I knew she heard me and was able to meet me where I was.

WALES, JULY 2020—AGE THIRTY-TWO
As I drove up the A470, I began to feel nervous. My mind started spurting out things like, *This is crazy. This is ridiculous. What are you doing? You should cancel.* What I know

now was that my small self, my ego, which had formed a thick protective shell around my trauma, was protesting. Another thick layer was facing its removal. I arrived at her house and parked out front.

I rang the doorbell, and a beautiful woman with sparkly blue eyes and long red hair answered the door. She wasn't wearing any shoes, and her floral dress floated around her legs. I felt an instant softening within my body in her presence.

She guided me to her treatment room where we talked further. She asked me questions about my childhood and about the way I had been feeling. We talked further about the eating disorder and the feelings, thoughts, and beliefs I held about my body. She said since it was our first session, she would get a feel for my energy body and be guided from there. I lay back on the couch and pulled the soft blanket over my legs as I closed my eyes and focused on my breathing.

A heat and a prickling sensation began at my feet, like a vacuum at my heels was pulling me down. I was sure my body was shaking and moving around the room, but when I opened my eyes a little, I saw I was still on the bed. Then in my mind's eye, red and orange colors swirled, and a voice, not unlike my own, but with a gentle wisdom I did not possess said, "There you are." In that moment, I felt as if someone had pulled a cork out of my heart. I perceived an opening, an expansion, and the entire universe rushed in and a great cry left my body.

I sobbed, howling, but my eyes remained shut as my body shook and a great stream of tears ran down my face onto my neck. Firm hands came to my shoulders. As I cried, my throat opened, my mouth relaxed, and I let out a noise that sounded like a call, a summoning, and a reclamation.

As my body stilled itself, I realized I was watching. I *was* the energy swirling, and I traveled for the first time around my body. To my womb, my sacral chakra, and there I saw the face of the babies that I would never hold. I saw the image of a Native American woman standing on the edge of a cliff holding a baby, an eagle flying over her head, and knew myself to be her. Her loss and her grief were nestled deep within my womb space. Then I saw a man, a Roman centurion, rise with his battle cry, and I knew him and his anger as he plunged his sword deep into his enemy.

Finally, I dove into all the sadness and grief as I swam into a dark cave and found a little girl. I saw the noose around her neck. I saw how she wanted to be brought out of the darkness. And when I looked down, I saw the end of the rope in my hand. I was trapping me, and all I had to do was untether myself.

CHAPTER 15

Sifting through Dead Bodies

―

The soul
Is indestructible

"Being good" was destroying me. Because in the "being good," I rejected any aspect of myself that did not fit into that category. I wanted only the light, but the light cannot illuminate without darkness. I adopted ideas about myself, collected identities, and did everything to be a version of myself that other people would love and accept. But eventually, the parts that were rooted in the truth of me rose, and they spoke with such rage and anger they had in them the fiery potential to burn everything to the ground.

I was continually running from the "not good" parts of myself. But everywhere I went, there they were. Not only in myself but mirrored back by everyone around me. Choosing to let go and create a boundary between me and my mother was not the solution. It was part of the transformation.

Forgetting about the other things that had happened to me and "moving on" was not going to eradicate the pain that still existed within and the stories I continued to spin for myself. It was my responsibility to dismantle the web once and for all.

AUSTRALIA, 1992—AGE FIVE

I walk down a rocky path as tall gum trees sway in the breeze. I look ahead and can see my parents. I trail behind slowly, keeping their backs in view. We are somewhere in the bush, and as I look up, I see the expansive, bowl-like blue sky reach far and wide. As I breathe in, I smell the red, dry, crackling earth below me. I become still, as a tingling sensation and then an inertia guides me to turn around. As I turn, I hear a voice from within, *Samala*, and my gaze moves to the ground. I see a glistening blue gem nestled between the dusty earth and rocks. As I bend to pick it up, I *feel* the words, "Samala, I am here." As I straighten, I smooth the stone between my fingers. Looking around, I can no longer see my parents, but I don't feel afraid.

I knew that voice then, and I know it now. Somewhere in between that moment and the beginning of 2020, I had forgotten who it belonged to. It was mine. The voice I have carried in me from the moment my soul joined my body in utero. That voice that had pulled me back from the edge of destruction was me, but not me as I had always thought of me. It was something bigger, something greater. And I remembered that I had always been held, and I would always be held.

WALES, JULY 2020—AGE THIRTY-TWO

As my journey with Sian and reiki began, other modes of healing and self-discovery opened before me. One after the other, like stepping stones, the next layer became visible. Books that I had purchased years before but had remained unread called to me. People who had existed on the peripheral of my life made their way into my awareness. The more I trusted in not knowing exactly *how* I was going to heal, the more I transformed and healed.

In the first session with Sian, I confirmed to myself what I already intuitively knew was happening. My consciousness was expanding, and I was awakening to the interconnectedness that was all around me and within me. My soul was calling, and it was calling loudly. The intense suffering had been the catalyst for my emergence. The thick cocoon of my mind had constricted me to the point that I had no choice but to shatter the chrysalis.

Curiosity overtook any fear. I was not afraid to face myself. Not unlike Bluebeard's wife, who when her husband departed for a time was given the keys for every door in the house and went into the only forbidden room against his orders. In that room, she found the cadavers of her hopes, dreams, and the exiled parts of herself piled on top of one another. He had promised her a life of joy and happiness, so long as she never faced her truth. And of course, on his return, he was not pleased, and she had to fight for her newfound awareness.

And my mind, out of protection, like Bluebeard had forbidden me to see my own truth. But when the tiny cracks had appeared and the curiosity grew with incredible strength, I began to wade and sift through the dead bodies. I had no choice but to bring everything out of the basement and to shine awareness on every shadow, every crevasse. To bring all of me into my heart. The anxiety, the eating disorder, and the stress were all masks, and behind them stood a wall of pain and fracture. Memories, perceptions, and beliefs were running the show, doing their best to keep me safe. And on the lowest level was me, my soul, my authenticity. Waiting.

As the pandemic of 2020 continued around me, I devoted myself to spiritual practice and to my healing. I devoted myself to uncovering who I truly was. Through that, I began to see the past differently. I began to see the threads that linked every experience. I went back, one by one, and relived them, allowed myself to weep, to get angry, and then to let go. I saw how each experience offered up deep wisdom and insight. I began to set boundaries and recognize when fear was arising. If I wanted to become the person I knew I was deep within, I had to begin to accept where I was in the moment.

In September 2020, a good friend and mentor of mine, Jenny Burrell, reached out to me. She was studying in a type of therapy called compassionate enquiry, which was developed by Dr. Gabor Mate. She was aware that I was moving through a transformation and asked if I would be interested in doing some sessions with her as part of her training. This type of therapy is a psychotherapeutic approach to healing complex trauma. Through our sessions together, we got in touch with my inner child, my fear of being seen, and uncovered the way I had adopted the eating disorder as a coping mechanism. While the work with Liz had given me a foundation to managing the eating disorder, through compassionate enquiry, I was able to listen to the parts of me that were driving the behavior.

Even after working with Liz and working with Sian, I had moments when I relapsed into a binge and purge pattern. When I came to work with Jenny for six weeks, we moved deeper into the heart of the pain. I was using my eating disorder to fire fight. Whenever I experienced an intense emotion, experienced boredom or unfulfillment, I would binge and purge. And it was addictive. The adrenaline during the binge, and the feeling of relief after the purge. A large element of shame was also attached to the eating disorder, so much so that even when I was working with Liz, I didn't completely accept it. When we delved into uncovering the trauma and the episodes lessened, I put the eating disorder to the side. But with Jenny, I was ready to go all the way into the depths of the eating disorder cycle.

Early on in our time together, she coached me through a session where I sat in a tent, in my mind, with the disowned parts of myself. And I listened to each of them. The eating disorder was a behavioral pattern that had been created to help—however unhelpful it might appear. Through that realization, I uncovered a great level of compassion toward myself. My eating disorder had protected me when I had needed it most. In times of great distress, when I had no other way of soothing the internal pain, it was there. But now it was time to find other, more nourishing ways to soothe and protect myself. I was able to let that part of me go with love. Ultimately, I learned that the continual ongoing experience of *not* revisiting my emotions and questioning the stories I held about myself was far more painful than the initial traumas themselves. What I was doing to myself and the ways in which I treated myself was worse than all the initial traumas.

As I neared the end of 2020, so much of my healing became about sitting with my inner child, little Samala, and offering up love to her. I would ask little me, "What do you want to do today?" For a long time, she didn't know, so many times in meditation she would sit on my lap, and I would simply brush her hair. Slowly, she began to trust me. And then the older versions of me presented themselves: tween me, teen me, and then finally, adult me, all waiting to be held and loved. I listened to their pain, their hurt, and their grief. I became capable of holding myself through the emotional storms when those parts of me were triggered into pain.

And with that came the recognition that I could be a different mother to my children. Where the world had seemed closed and dark to me, my view shifted to it being full of possibility and light. I could be myself with my children. I could let go, I could play, and I could open my heart. But I could also be responsible and firm while setting boundaries. And most of all, I could sit with their pain, their emotional outbursts, and hold them without needing to disconnect from myself.

As I neared the end of my sessions with Jenny, the pivotal shift was no longer seeing myself as anyone's victim. My perspective changed to seeing that every act of violence toward me reflected the deep pain that existed within that individual. With that came an understanding about what forgiveness really meant. I had never truly understood forgiveness. I had grown up believing that forgiveness was for the other person.

And in the interest of being a "good person," you forgive another person when they hurt you.

But in fact, the forgiveness was for *me*. And I did not have to forgive if I didn't want to. But for as long as I held onto my unforgiveness, I was tethered to them energetically and emotionally. I also realized that I could forgive and not be in a relationship with that person. But there are layers to forgiveness, and I wasn't going to rush myself through the process. I trusted that when my heart was ready, it would let me know.

We all have a choice to heal and to forgive ourselves and others for the things done out of pain. And the first step of forgiveness was turning it toward myself. While I would not wish any of my experiences on anyone, they have been my greatest lessons. My mother, my father, and the people who have presented the biggest challenges in my life thus far have been my greatest teachers. And most importantly, by consciously bringing everything out of the shadows, I can choose not to pass this lineage onto my children. Through my healing journey, I can see how it is possible for us to break the wheel of the stories, behaviors, and psychological patterns we inherit.

Deepening my understanding of self, of how the mind works, and of how the body holds trauma, I was able to begin to shift my perception of being unlovable and of being unworthy. And while I am still working on the deeper layers, I now know it is possible to change any story—about ourselves or another. None of it is set in stone. At the beginning of 2020, my true self, my authentic self, was buried underneath the stories and beliefs I held about myself. But just as diamonds are formed under intense pressure, my truest self was waiting to be uncovered. And she is fierce and brave with an open heart.

WALES, MAY 2021—AGE THIRTY-THREE

Trees dissolve into a green haze as I run down the trail. I move my body faster, keeping time to the beat of the music in my headphones. The air on my face is cold, as is the air against the back of my throat. My attention turns to my breath and then to a building sensation in my chest. Everything around me dissolves, and I sense my energy expand outward. Bliss permeates my entire being. I sense it all, the web of connectivity to the invisible field around me. A whisper from within. The next step.

Forgive.

EPILOGUE

Unfurling

Slowly
Opening
Unfurling
Expanding
Going wider
Diving deeper
Breathing space around
All that I am

What you have read is the beginning and the ending. A letting go. A death of who I believed I was. Over the past two years, and even in the past eight months of writing this book, I have moved past barriers I could not have believed possible, making way for forgiveness and evolution. My desire is to bring my whole self online. To embrace and express the light and the dark. Surrendering to being the human and the soul. There is nowhere to go. There is no arrival. I have always been *whole*.

When I began my journey in 2020, I did indeed believe there was an endpoint. And while, yes, I have transcended so much and no longer suffer with chronic anxiety, an eating disorder, or many of the complex trauma symptoms I was experiencing, I am still doing "the work." But it has taken on a different form. I am moving deeper into myself. Just like the spiral, I have moved outward, and now I am returning inward, to home, to center. I am working with a coach, Brad, who is facilitating my next layer of growth, harmonizing unbalanced perceptions, and restoring balance to my nervous system as I return to center. I am in the crux of a deeper transformation. And the past two years built the foundation for me to do this work.

WALES, AUGUST 2022—AGE THIRTY-FIVE
I lay on the bottom bunk in my daughter's bed.

Tears roll down my face, and my eyes close tightly. I am revisiting that moment again; I am by the roadside. I am three again. I am all alone. The memory is still heavy, but I feel an indifference to it.

"Samala, you're there. You're at the roadside. You're standing there, perceiving yourself as all alone. What else is there? What are you learning in that moment?" Brad's voice is gentle but firm, coming through my phone that lies next to me.

I feel a building sensation in my body. I'm almost there. The memory becomes alive. And I sense it. The truth.

"It's the first time… I connected to self. There's inner silence. Like, after she left, I was scared… I was afraid… but then I wasn't… Because I felt my self… My knowing… That was the first time I felt it."

"And in that moment, what were you being shown? What were you learning?"

The words come from within me, through my body, out of my mouth, and my heart. It opens.

"I was building strength. And I was learning… about home. I was learning that I was, and always will be, *home*."

Tears of gratitude slide down my face, and I begin to laugh.

==

THE END. AND
THE BEGINNING

Acknowledgments

I would like to thank Cristin Collins for introducing me to Eric Koester and the amazing team at The Creators Institute and, of course, New Degrees Press.

The story you have just read would not have been possible without the support, wisdom, and guidance of my editors, Katie Sigler and Megan Hart.

To my sisters, my dad, and my nanna.

To the baristas in Waterloo tea rooms for supplying me with endless coffee and cake.

To everyone who has been a part of my transformation journey and held space for my healing and answered my endless amounts of questions—especially Jane, Sian Cecil, Jenny Burrell, Cora Darlington, and Brad Holmes.

A very special thank you to my Authors Community—Darcie Bygraves, Danielle Bastier, Rachel Charles, Sian Walden, Camille Naismith, Jeni Law, Helen Golten, Sian Cecil, Cristin

Collins, Eric Koester, Max Bygraves, Stephanie Harries, Rachel Cox, Amy Morgan, Phil Simpson, Hannah Follet, Dominique Guishard, Angharad Era, Chris Sudworth, Max Bygraves, Sinead Singh, Oxsana Gorluck, Amanda Thompson, Sara Taylor, El Higgins, Vanessa Kerai, Clare Jones, Eleanor Dart, Katie Guy, Helen Tomlins, Abi Coop, Lisa Thompson, Helen Kerrigan, Emma Crook, Farishna Chohan, Cerys Ponting, Renee Cassleman, Jevgenija Triantafillu, and Tanya Valor for believing in and supporting the publishing of *Spiral*.

And everyone else who has offered up kind words, a listening ear, and the strength to continue writing when I felt I couldn't.

And to my mum. While the journey has been challenging for both of us, you have been my greatest teacher.

Lastly, thank you, dear reader, thank you for reading my story.

www.ingramcontent.com/pod-product-compliance
Lightning Source LLC
LaVergne TN
LVHW010322070526
838199LV00065B/5632